I0450384

Status Report for the National Wetlands Inventory Program: 2009

U.S. Fish and Wildlife Service
Division of Habitat and Resource Conservation
Branch of Resource and Mapping Support
Arlington, Virginia 22203

October 2009

PROGRAM CONTACTS - U.S. FISH AND WILDLIFE SERVICE

David Stout
Chief, Division of Habitat and Resource Conservation
U.S. Fish and Wildlife Service
4401 North Fairfax Drive
Arlington, VA 22203-1610
(703) 358-2278

Marty Kodis
Chief, Branch of Resource and Mapping Support
U.S. Fish and Wildlife Service
4401 North Fairfax Drive
Arlington, VA 22203-1610
(703) 358-2161

For other NWI contacts, check web at: http://www.fws.gov/wetlands/Organization/staff.html

Table of Contents

Acknowledgments

The leadership for the program provided by past project leaders – John Montanari and Donald Woodard – and all the work done by a large cadre of photointerpreters and cartographers (too numerous to mention individually) working on the project at the National Wetlands Inventory Center (St. Petersburg, Florida) and in the regions through the NWI's 30-year history are greatly appreciated. Also former regional wetland coordinators are recognized for their efforts to move the NWI from its infancy to where we are today: Dennis Peters (Region 1), Warren Hagenbuck and David Dall (Region 2), Ron Erickson and Kim Santos (Region 3), John Hefner and Charles Storrs (Region 4), Charles Elliott (Region 6), and Arthur Laperriere, Jon Hall, and Bill Pearson (Region 7). Special thanks go to all the agencies and organizations that have contributed to the NWI in various ways to the success of the NWI (Appendix B). The editor, Ralph Tiner, expresses his gratitude for the material and peer review of the draft provided by the NWI's regional, Washington Office, and Madison Office personnel: Bill Kirchner, Jim Dick, Brian Huberty, John Swords, Kevin Bon, Jerry Tande, Bill Wilen, Jo Ann Mills, and Tom Dahl, and for the maps and data provided by Mitch Bergeson and Julie Michaelson. This report would not have been possible without their contributions.

Executive Summary

The National Wetlands Inventory Program (NWI) has been producing wetland maps and geospatial wetland data for the United States since the mid-1970s. The focus on the program has been on two fronts: 1) map or digital database preparation and delivery to the public, and 2) projecting and reporting on national wetland trends using a probability-based sampling design. The status of mapping has been made available through various media throughout the program's 30-year history (e.g., state atlases, regional status maps, and now through the internet via the Wetlands Mapper online tool). Annual progress reports have been produced for internal uses, but the NWI has never produced a national status report for public distribution. Given the evolution of the NWI, the diversity of products and activities with which the program is involved, and the wide public use of our products, the NWI decided to prepare this first status report. Being the first such report, it provides an introduction to the NWI Program in addition to reporting on the annual progress and activities across the regions. Future annual reports will focus on yearly accomplishments.

The NWI has produced wetland data for more than 90 percent of the conterminous United States, the entire state of Hawaii, and nearly 30 percent of Alaska. This work was done with the cooperation of other agencies including the Corps of Engineers, EPA, numerous states, and several universities. Prior to budget cuts exacted in 1996, the NWI was generating wetland data at a rate that covered as much as 10 percent of the lower 48 states per year. Today the annual production rate is down to about 1-2 percent. Consequently, most of the data were derived from mid-1980s imagery, so the data in many areas do not reflect current conditions, especially

in places where much development or natural change has occurred over the past 20 years. Yet even where the information is dated, many, if not most, of the wetlands mapped by NWI still remain in one form or another. Today's improved mapping techniques, however, allow for better wetland detection, so that more wetlands can be found and better boundaries delineated. Some states have initiated wetland inventories that are being used to update the NWI data. However this is not the case nationwide as many states still lack current wetland data and the resources to update NWI data. Emerging conservation issues related to global climate change (including sea-level rise, storm flooding, and drought) and domestic energy development have heightened the need for updated (more real-time) wetlands data. Applications of NWI data include use in: 1) predicting the impacts of sea-level rise, 2) wetland restoration planning, 3) planning for energy independence (primarily in the West and Alaska), 4) analyzing carbon sequestration in wetlands, 5) landscape-level or watershed-based wetland characterizations and functional assessments, 6) planning and management for National Wildlife Refuges (including targeting areas for acquisition) and other federal lands, 7) planning, modeling, research, and monitoring for Strategic Habitat Conservation work by the Service, 8) recovery planning for endangered species, fish, migratory birds, marine mammals, and other imperiled species, and 9) invasive species management.

In the mid-1970s, the creators of NWI thought the inventory would be done in a few years given their vision of the inventory as a broad-brushed survey of wetlands (1:250,000 scale). When the direction was changed to produce a more comprehensive inventory by producing maps at a

scale of 1:24,000, it was clear that the inventory would not be completed in the near future. To meet the needs for answering the question of how much wetland is there in the Nation, the NWI developed a statistically based national wetland status and trend (NWST) study. Using data from 3,635 four-square mile plots, the NWST study generated estimates of major wetland types and reported on wetland trends from the mid-1950s to the mid-1970s. This study found that 458,000 acres of wetlands were lost annually during this 20-year period. Two publications were written on these findings, one reporting the results (acreage summaries of the status and trends; Frayer et al. 1983) and the other describing the diversity of wetland types across the country, their values, the impacts of these changes on wildlife and other wetland functions, and current threats (Tiner 1984). The combination of these reports educated policy-makers and the public on the status and threats to the Nation's wetlands and the significance of these losses and was instrumental in influencing public policy and helping improve wetland conservation. Subsequent national status and trend reports covered the mid-70s to mid-80s, and every decade thereafter. The NWI now receives some funding from other agencies (Corps of Engineers, Environmental Protection Agency, Natural Resources Conservation Service, and National Oceanic and Atmospheric Administration-National Marine Fisheries Service) to conduct these assessments. The next national trends study is scheduled for completion in FY2010.

While the focus of the NWI has been on producing wetland data (maps and geospatial data), our partners have been interested in having us prepare a variety of related products. They have provided funds to develop special products that include riparian habitat inventories, regional and local wetland trends reports, watershed-based wetland characterization and preliminary functional assessment reports, reports on the natural habitat integrity of watersheds, and inventories of potential wetland and riparian restoration sites. These products have become part of the suite of products that the NWI can provide on an as-needed and as-funded basis.

The NWI Program has come a long way since its beginnings in the mid-1970s. It is much more than a mapping operation, providing data and analyses that allow decision-makers to make better informed decisions on the fate of wetlands and that have helped educate the American public on wetlands, their values, status, and threats.

Photo Credit: Ralph Tiner, USFWS

Introduction

Wetlands are the cornerstone of the Nation's most ecologically and economically important ecosystems. They benefit fish, wildlife, and people. The National Wetlands Inventory Program (NWI) was established in the 1970s to provide valuable information on the status of wetlands to decision-makers for making more informed decisions on the fate of these vital natural resources. While the NWI has produced annual progress reports for internal administrative purposes, this is the first status report produced to describe program accomplishments for agencies, organizations, and others outside the Service. The report begins with a brief overview of the NWI that describes how the program has changed over the years. The overview is followed by a review of the status of the NWI in each region, coordination activities, a summary of some interesting uses of NWI products, and a list of major regional wetland publications produced by the NWI for the region. This report provides specific information on the regional activities of the NWI Program. A separate annual report on the activities of the National Standards and Support Group has been prepared (U.S. Fish and Wildlife Service 2009). That report focuses on the status of the wetlands master geospatial database including data collection, contributed data, and its relation to the U.S. Geological Survey's National Map, Geo-spatial One Stop, and Data.gov.

Photo Credit: Ralph Tiner, USFWS

Overview of the NWI Program
By Ralph Tiner

Background[1]

The National Wetlands Inventory (NWI) Program was established by the Service in 1974 to conduct a nationwide inventory of U.S. wetlands to provide its biologists and others with information on the distribution of wetlands to aid in wetland conservation efforts. To do this, the NWI developed a wetland classification system (Cowardin et al. 1979) which is now both the official Service wetland classification system and the federal standard for wetland classification (adopted by the Federal Geographic Data Committee on July 29, 1996: 61 Federal Register 39465). The NWI also had to develop techniques for mapping and recording the inventory findings. The NWI relies on trained photointerpreters (image analysts) to interpret wetlands and deepwater habitats from aerial photography or digital aerial imagery. The NWI started mapping wetlands at a small scale (1:250,000 map which covers an area the size of 128-1:24,000 USGS topographic maps or approximately 7,400 square miles). Service field personnel were not satisfied with this product so eventually large-scale (1:24K) maps became the standard product delivered by the program. As computer mapping technology evolved, the NWI maps were digitized for geographic information system (GIS) applications. In the mid-1990s due to budget cuts and technology innovations, the NWI discontinued production of paper maps in favor of distributing NWI data via online "mapping tools" where people could make custom maps for their area of interest. Today, the NWI serves its data up on a variety of base maps through a tool called the "Wetlands Mapper" and on a current aerial image via a link to Google Earth (see examples in "Products" section). GIS users can also connect their application to real-time data directly through an online wetland mapping service or download NWI data for their own applications (maps, data analyses, and reports). Data can be downloaded by quad or by state. The techniques used by the NWI have recently been adopted by the Federal Geographic Data Committee as the federal wetland mapping standard (FGDC Wetlands Subcommittee 2009). This standard will be applied to all federal grants involving wetland mapping to insure that such mapping by states and others can be added to the NWI's wetlands master geospatial database.

How Mapping Techniques Have Changed

The mapping techniques of the NWI have also evolved over time. At the outset, the NWI produced maps by first interpreting wetlands and deepwater habitats from high-altitude aerial photography (including 1:130,000, 1:80,000, and 1:62,500 photos). Acetate overlays were attached to the aerial photos and the interpreter outlined and labeled wetlands and deepwater habitats with pen and ink (Figure 1). Data from the overlays were then transferred by cartographers to mylar overlays attached to a standard topographic map (e.g., 1:24,000 for lower 48 states and Hawaii, and 1:63,360 for Alaska). Small-scale maps including 1:100,000 maps were then made by cartographers through an engraving process. The final step would be digitizing data from large-scale NWI maps to create a geospatial database. As GIS and mapping technology advanced, the process of data collection and map production became an integrated operation (single step) done on-screen by the photointerpreter. Interpreters delineated wetlands onscreen and data were simultaneously entered into a digital data layer that could be used to generate maps at various scales using GIS technology. Today, nearly all of the NWI data are created through this on-screen process. This technology also

Figure 1. Interpretation of aerial photographs using stereoscope, acetate overlays, pen and ink, and collateral data.

---

[1] For more background information on the NWI Program, consult: "National Wetlands Inventory: A Strategy for the 21st Century" (U.S. Fish and Wildlife Service 2002).

facilitated use of other sources in the interpretation process as other digital datasets (e.g., USDA soil survey geographic database and USGS national hydrography datasets) could be viewed with the source imagery to identify areas where wetlands are likely to be based on the presence of hydric soils, for example. The bulk of the NWI mapping was done by private contractors and universities (e.g., University of Massachusetts, South Dakota State University, Texas Tech, and Virginia Tech). In the Midwest, Ducks Unlimited has recently been contracted to do NWI mapping.

How NWI Products Have Changed

Through most of the NWI's history large-scale wetland maps were the prime product (Figure 2). Today the basic products are: 1) wetlands master geospatial database that can be used to generate maps and statistics about the status of the Nation's wetlands and 2) the national wetlands status and trends reports derived from data collected from four-square mile plots. The NWI has also produced a variety of reports summarizing the results of its work for regional and local geographic areas.

Wetland Map Data. NWI geospatial data are available via the internet (http://www.fws.gov/wetlands) and individuals can produce custom maps showing NWI data on planimetric maps (Figure 3) or on aerial imagery using a link to Google Earth (Figure 4) or on topographic maps (Figure 5) using the USGS National Map Viewer (http://nmviewogc.cr.usgs.gov/viewer.htm). The Service is responsible for producing and maintaining the wetlands layer of the National Spatial Data Infrastructure which is a major component of the Department of Interior's geospatial line of business portfolio and E-government through the Geospatial One-Stop Initiative and "The National Map" and as a standards-compliant layer on the new data.gov.

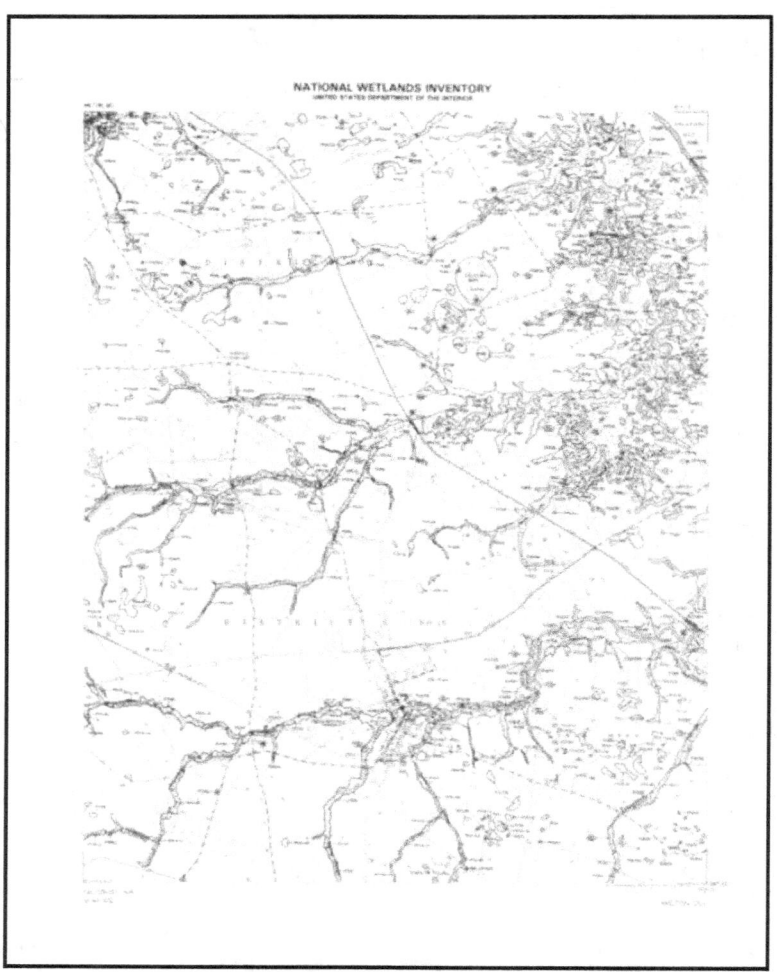

Figure 2. Example of 1:24K NWI map – Milton, DE quadrangle. (Note: Legend has been deleted for this figure.)

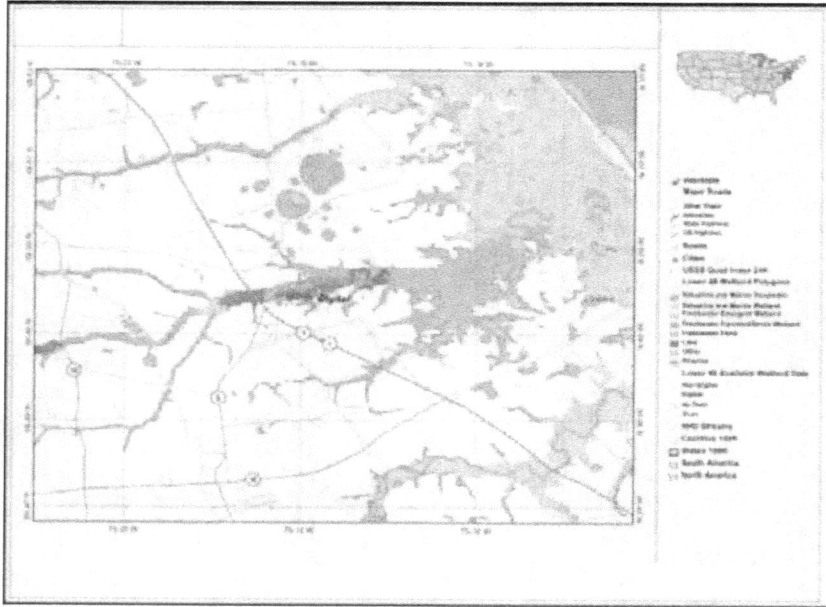

Figure 3. Example of custom NWI map made from the "Wetlands Mapper." This map covers the area around Milton, DE - a portion of the area shown in Figure 2.

Figure 4. NWI data displayed on Google Earth image for the Milton, DE area.

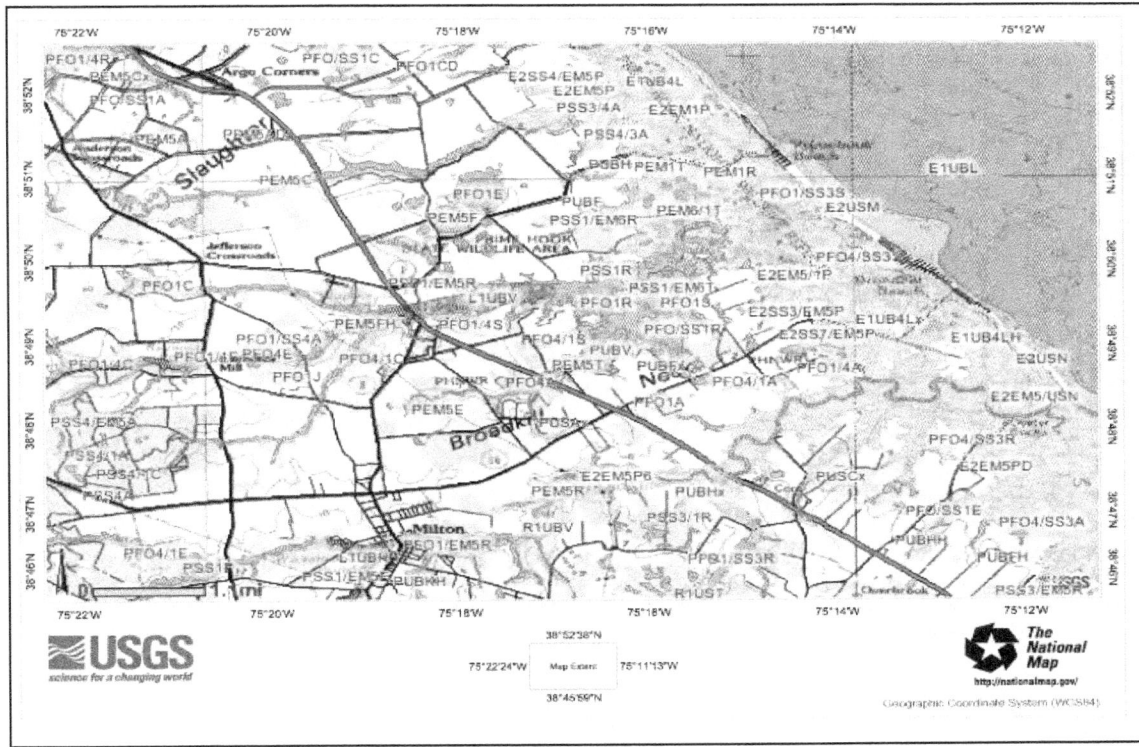

Figure 5. NWI data displayed on a USGS topographic map using the National Map Viewer for the Milton, DE area.

NWI Reports. Reporting the findings of the actual mapping has been inadequate to date; only in the Northeast Region have such reports been routinely published (e.g., state wetland reports summarizing the mapping results). The NWI also has prepared "special project reports" for work often funded by outside agencies including local and regional wetland trend reports, local wetland status reports, watershed-based wetland characterization and preliminary functional assessment reports, coastal submerged aquatic vegetation inventory reports, and watershed-based reports on natural habitat integrity (see section "Beyond Standard NWI Mapping – Special Projects"). A sample list of the various types of NWI reports published to date is given in the Appendix A. Many of the reports are now online and can be searched on the NWI website (http://www.fws.gov/wetlands/) using the "Documents Search Engine" (type in subject of interest); some may also be accessed online at the Service's Conservation Library (http://library.fws.gov/WetlandPublications.html). The NWI will be placing more emphasis on summarizing the results of their work and many reports will be published in 2010 and beyond.

Why the National Wetland Status and Trend Study Was Started

Initially, the creators of NWI thought the inventory would be done in a few years given their vision of the inventory as a broad-brushed survey of wetlands (1:250,000 scale). When the direction was changed to produce a more comprehensive inventory by producing maps at a scale of 1:24,000, it was rather obvious that the inventory would not be completed in the near future. To meet the needs for answering the question of how much wetland is there in the Nation, the NWI developed a statistically based national wetland status and trend (NWST) study. Using data from 3,635 four-square mile plots, the NWST study generated estimates of major wetland types and reported

on wetland trends from the mid-1950s to the mid-1970s. This study found that 458,000 acres of wetlands were lost annually during this 20-year period. Two publications were written on these findings, one reporting the results (acreage summaries of the status and trends; Frayer et al. 1983) and the other describing the diversity of wetland types across the country, their values, the impacts of these changes on wildlife and other wetland functions, and current threats (Tiner 1984). The combination of these reports educated policy-makers and the public on the status and threats to the Nation's wetlands and the significance of these losses and was instrumental in influencing public policy and helping improve wetland conservation. Subsequent national status and trend reports covered the mid-70s to mid-80s, and every decade since as authorized by the Emergency Wetland Resources Act of 1986 (Dahl and Johnson 1991, Dahl 2000, and Dahl 2006).[2] The NWI now receives some funding from other agencies (Corps of Engineers, Environmental Protection Agency, Natural Resources Conservation Service, and National Oceanic and Atmospheric Administration-National Marine Fisheries Service) to conduct these assessments.

The next national trends study is scheduled for completion in FY2010.

Where We Are Today in Mapping the Nation's Wetlands

The maps below shows the status of the NWI across the country and the date of the imagery used to produce the data (Figures 7 and 8). Over the past 30 years, the NWI has produced wetland data for most of the county, with digital data available for about 61 percent of the country.

As can be seen in Figure 8, the effective date of the NWI for most of the coterminous U.S. is 1980s (mostly derived from mid-1980s 1:58,000 color infrared photos), with substantial areas based on 1970s imagery (1:80,000 black and white photos). From the 1991 to 1996, the NWI was producing data for 5% of the lower 48 states per year. Today, NWI data are being updated by the Service at a rate of 1-2% per year with the help of outside partners. The program has averaged this slower rate since receiving a 50% budget cut in 1996 done in a response to the Administration's effort to reduce the federal deficit. This action severely reduced the funding available for mapping work (funding available for actual mapping declined from about

Figure 6. NWI produced two reports from its first national wetland status and trends study.

---

[2] This Act also established a target for completing nationwide mapping for the lower 48 states by September 30, 1998 and for Alaska by September 30, 2000 but adequate funding to do this was never authorized; in fact the NWI budget was reduced by about 50% in 1996 as part of a government-wide effort to reduce federal spending and eliminate the federal deficit.

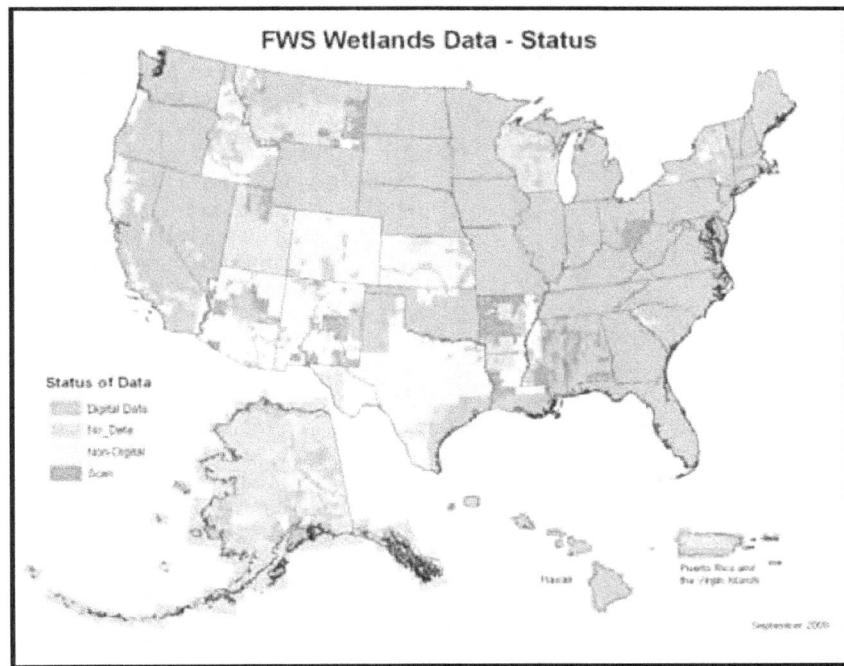

Figure 7. Status of NWI data for the country. Non-digital data are hardcopy maps or interpreted photo-overlays, while scans represent data scanned from hardcopy maps for use on the Wetlands Mapper.

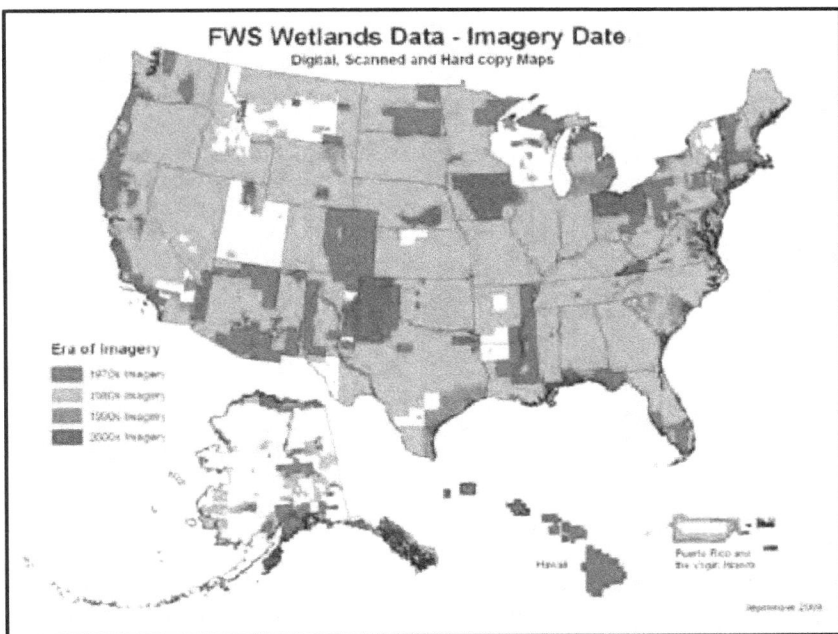

Figure 8. Era of imagery used for NWI; the white areas have not been mapped.

$5M to $1.5M) and significantly compromised the NWI's ability to produce contemporary wetland data. Funding devoted to the Service's map production was also low in both 2008 and again in 2009 as the program focused on producing the analysis for the national wetland status and trends report due in 2010. Since the NWI is not producing

wetlands data at the rate it was in its early years, a number of states have taken the initiative to produce their own wetland inventory for priority areas. In July 2009, the Federal Geographic Data Committee established a federal wetland mapping standard that requires agencies receiving federal funds for such efforts to follow; this will insure

that new wetland data produced with federal dollars will be collected in a format ready for entering into the national wetlands master geospatial database (Federal Geographic Data Committee 2009).

Who Has Contributed to the NWI?

Over the past 30 years, the NWI has had many cooperators in conducting the inventory. Some partners have provided funding to perform the surveys, some conduct the surveys, some participate by reviewing draft NWI data, while others distribute NWI data. Cooperators include states, other federal agencies, tribal governments, regional and local governments, and nonprofit organizations (Appendix B). We have also received funding from other Service programs to map wetlands including the Prairie Pothole Joint Venture, Partners for Fish and Wildlife, and the National Wildlife Refuge Program. Partners in 2009 include the states of Oregon, Oklahoma, Montana, and Wisconsin as well as the Bureau of Land Management, the Forest Service, Tennessee Valley Authority, and Ducks Unlimited. These partners provided for 85 percent of the data added to the Wetlands Mapper this year.

How the NWI Budget Has Changed

The NWI budget has risen and fallen since 1975 and has flattened at around $5M (Figure 9). In 1986, the program received roughly a $1M boost, while in 1992, a $3M increase occurred. These increases provided income that was dedicated strictly to mapping, leading to substantial increases in map production and cost-sharing from other agencies (Figure 10). In 1996, the NWI budget was reduced by about 50% which severely hampered the program's ability to keep NWI maps up-to-date and to produce original mapping for unmapped areas. For FY2009, the NWI budget was $5.3 million. Nearly $3.7M was required to pay salary, space, equipment, and Washington Office overhead to keep the program running, leaving $1.6M for projects. Of the latter, more than half of the "mapping funds" were dedicated to conducting the 10-year

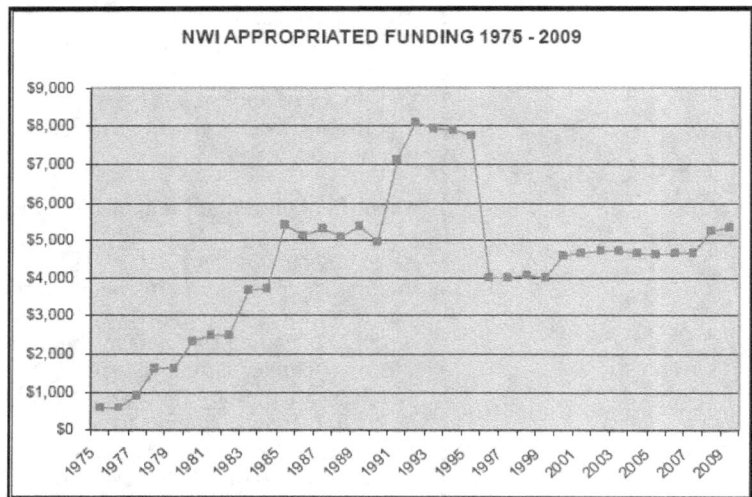

Figure 9. Appropriated funding for NWI since 1975.

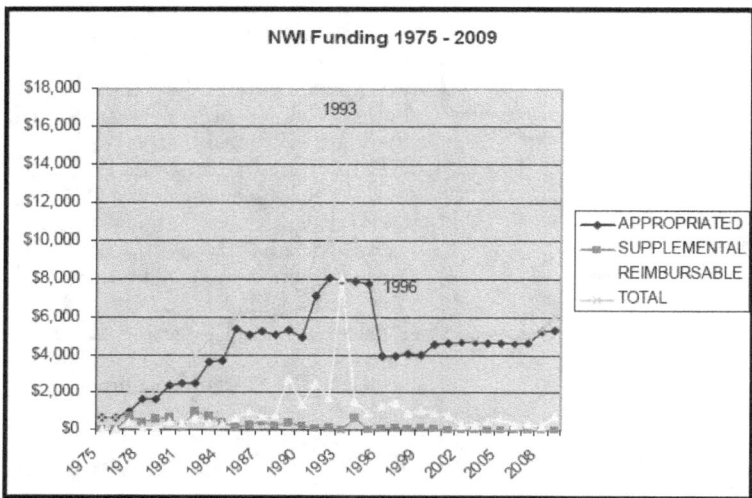

Figure 10. Funding for the NWI including reimbursable funding from other sources since 1975. Dollar amounts are in thousands of dollars (e.g., $8,000 = $8,000,000). This graph does not include funds secured by individual regions for NWI mapping and special projects where contracts were processed through the regions. (Note: These figures do not include reimbursable funding received by the Service from other federal agencies for two national wetland status and trend studies ($1.8M in 2004-5 and $800K in 2008-9).

national wetland trends analysis ($875K), leaving $725K available for regional mapping projects. Once the 2010 trends project is completed more funding will be allocated to wetland mapping. The NWI has identified over $100 million in projects for updating areas where current data are needed to meet Service priorities.

How NWI Data Are Used Across the Country

While habitat degradation and destruction from traditional sources continue, emerging conservation issues related to global climate change (including sea-level rise, storm flooding, and drought) and domestic energy development have heightened the need for updated (more real-time) wetlands data. Applications of NWI data include use in: 1) predicting the impacts of sea-level rise, 2) wetland restoration planning, 3) planning for energy independence (primarily in the West and Alaska), 4) analyzing carbon sequestration in wetlands, 5) landscape-level or watershed-based wetland characterizations and functional assessments, 6) planning and management for National Wildlife Refuges (including targeting areas for acquisition) and

other federal lands, 7) planning, modeling, research, and monitoring for Strategic Habitat Conservation work by the Service, 8) recovery planning for endangered species, fish, migratory birds, marine mammals, and other imperiled species, and 9) invasive species management. General uses of NWI data are summarized below; see regional status reports for specific examples.

Wetland Protection and Management. The general public consults NWI data on a daily basis via the NWI website (Wetlands Mapper and Google Earth) when considering land purchases and development. Landowners, developers, real estate agents, and environmental consultants review NWI data as a first step in assessing the potential restrictions of land for residential, commercial, and industrial development. The U.S. Army Corps of Engineers uses NWI data during its permit review process (e.g., cumulative effects determinations and potential sites for mitigation banking) and includes a link to NWI data on its online permit tracking system (Figure 11). A national association of pesticide developers uses NWI data to reduce the effects of their products on wetland habitats.

Climate Change Impact Analysis. An important use of NWI data has arisen from concern about the impacts of climate change. The EPA-developed Sea-Level Affecting Marshes Model (SLAMM) predicts the possible effects of sea-level rise on coastal wetlands and adjacent lowlands. This model uses NWI data plus information on local topography, accretion and erosion rates, dikes, and development in making these predictions. SLAMM has been run for a few large estuaries including Puget Sound, Chesapeake Bay, and Delaware Bay and for numerous National Wildlife Refuges along the Atlantic, Gulf, and Pacific Coasts (Figure 12). The Service plans to apply SLAMM to all coastal refuges to aid in planning acquisition and management. Some existing applications are posted online by the Service's Chesapeake Bay Field Office (http://www.fws.gov/

slamm/; for additional information, see summary of Washington Office activities in this report). Since rising sea level threatens the integrity of dikes forming coastal waterfowl impoundments, refuge managers are using SLAMM and other data to formulate a strategy for determining when to keep maintaining the dikes and when to abandon such structures. Climate change will also pose significant consequences for inland wetlands with predicted shifts in precipitation patterns. NWI data are being used to quantify loss of wetlands in the prairie pothole region attributed to predicted drought in the upper Midwest. These declines will affect populations of waterfowl, shorebirds, and endangered species, and also could have a major impact on farmers, food security, and biofuels development. Since wetlands store carbon, wetland restoration can be important in reducing carbon dioxide concentrations in the atmosphere. Dr. Ed Nater (University of Minnesota) has used NWI data to help quantify carbon stored on wetlands. Restored farmed wetlands may form the basis for carbon-credit trading to mitigate greenhouse emissions from other sources that affect global climates. Existing NWI data serve as a starting point to identify potential restoration sites (farmed wetlands and former wetlands when used in combination with soil data) as well as to monitor carbon sinks for purposes of meeting future carbon sequestration needs.

Emergency Planning and Recovery. The Federal Emergency Management Agency (FEMA) and state agencies use NWI data to assist in the remediation and planning after hurricane disasters. The NWI Program partnered with the U.S. Geological Survey's National Wetlands Research Center to convert existing NWI maps to digital data and update the information for Louisiana for use by federal, state, and local agencies in recovery and planning efforts. This new information will also be used for a myriad of other purposes to help protect wetlands and wetland-dependent or associated wildlife, fish, and plant species. In May 2006, the Service

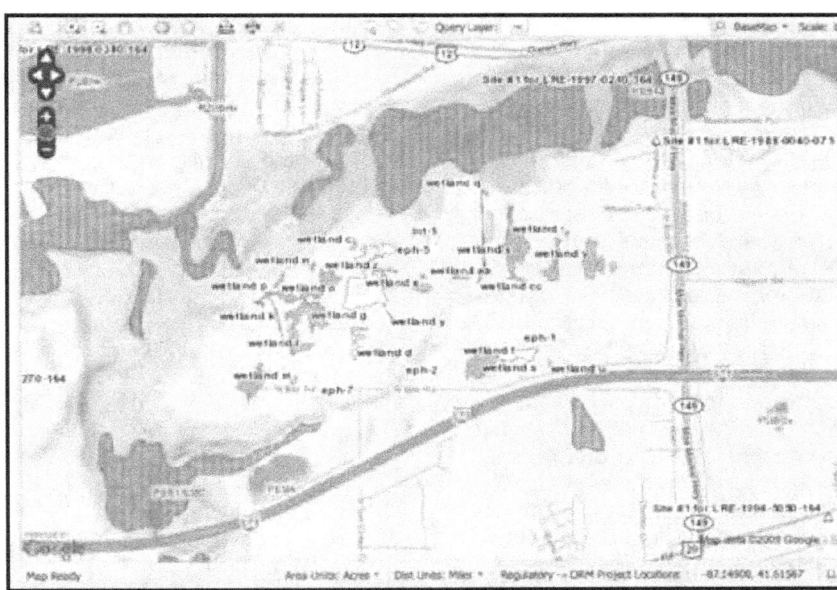

Figure 11. NWI data are integrated into the Corps' permit tracking system. Green areas = NWI wetlands, blue areas = NWI deepwater habitats, and pink and white areas = Corps field-verified wetlands in a project area. The latter wetlands were mostly below the target mapping unit; the dark green wetland below I-94 is 3.3 acres in size.

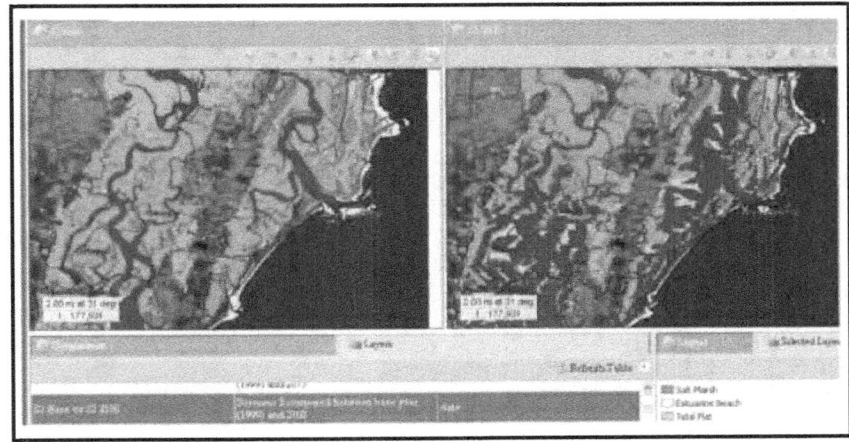

Figure 12. SLAMM uses NWI data to identify wetlands and marsh elevations for predicting and displaying the effects of sea-level rise in coastal regions: Year 2000 conditions (left) and Year 2100 conditions (right); note inundation of former coastal marshes.

responded to a request from the Center for Disease Control and the U.S. Department of Agriculture's Centers for Epidemiology and Animal Health (APHIS) related to avian influenza (bird flu). Because of the human health threats posed by a potential pandemic, infectious disease specialists wanted to develop a model to assess the threat level based on transmission of avian influenza virus spread through wild populations of migratory waterfowl and other water birds. To conduct these analyses, disease specialists needed to know where and how many wetlands and surface water

bodies might serve as staging areas for migrating birds. They requested the Service's assistance in acquiring digital NWI data from the Service's wetlands master geospatial database. The Service accessed and provided its entire wetlands digital dataset for the conterminous United States (40+ gigabytes) for the avian influenza study on May 30, 2006. APHIS will use this information to develop models of areas susceptible to avian influenza outbreaks should migratory bird populations become infected. This may have consequences for the deployment of emergency response medical teams and supplies should large numbers of birds become infected along migratory routes in close proximity to human population centers.

Wildlife Management and Conservation. Since an estimated 46% of endangered or threatened species are associated with wetlands, NWI data (including riparian habitat data for western states) is being used to help determine occurrence of species and design plans for species recovery. Certain NWI codes may be used to identify potential habitat for some species, or could be used in combination with other data to locate such habitat (see regional status sections for some examples of these applications). Waterfowl management is a major focus of the Service and the Prairie Pothole Region (PPR) is the Nation's premier waterfowl production area. NWI data have been used to produce breeding pair accessibility maps (aka "Thunderstorm Maps") for the PPR. These maps display predictions of the number of upland nesting duck pairs that could potentially nest in the upland portion of every 40-acre block of the PPR of Minnesota and Iowa. These predictions are based on the known maximum travel distances of hens from wetlands to their nest sites and regressions (statistical models) created from four-square mile survey data predicting the number of duck pairs that utilize every individual wetland in the PPR during a "typical" breeding

season (Figure 13). The maps are used to help identify priority sites for the protection or restoration of grassland habitats for breeding waterfowl, but are also useful in identifying priority wetland complexes to be protected through acquisition and easements, or to be enhanced by private lands wetland restorations. Sixteen states, Guam, and the Virgin Islands have identified NWI data as needed information for wildlife conservation planning (GA, IL, KS, MA, MI, MN, MT, NV, NH, NM, NY, OH, PA, TX, VA, and WV).

Aid to Other Mapping Efforts. The NWI data have been used by numerous agencies and academic institutions as base data for identifying wetlands for a host of remote sensing applications. Data have been used to assist investigators in performing supervised and unsupervised classification of wetlands as part of regional or national inventories of land use and land cover. For example, NOAA's C-CAP Program that produces data and maps showing changes in coastal watersheds uses NWI data to aid in detecting wetlands on satellite imagery. Similarly, university researchers have used NWI data in testing more local or site-specific applications of remote sensing technologies. NWI data has provided a foundation for more detailed wetland mapping in some

states and local areas. For example, the State of Delaware relied heavily on NWI data when updating wetland data for a statewide wetland database and essentially updated the NWI with more current imagery.

Biggest User Complaint about NWI data: We have heard from numerous users across the country that while they still use NWI data where it is the only source of wetland data available, the main complaint is that the data are too old for many applications and that the NWI data should be updated more frequently. In areas where more recent wetland data are available from state or other sources, NWI data are no longer used, except in a historical context.

Beyond Standard NWI Mapping - Special Products

The NWI through existing staff and mapping contractors have the skills and technology to do more than produce standard NWI data and wetland status and trends analyses. To meet the needs of our cooperators for additional wetland and related habitat information, we have developed a few other products. These products include riparian habitat classification and mapping, enhanced NWI mapping, landscape-level wetland functional assessments, potential wetland restoration site inventories, and natural habitat integrity indices

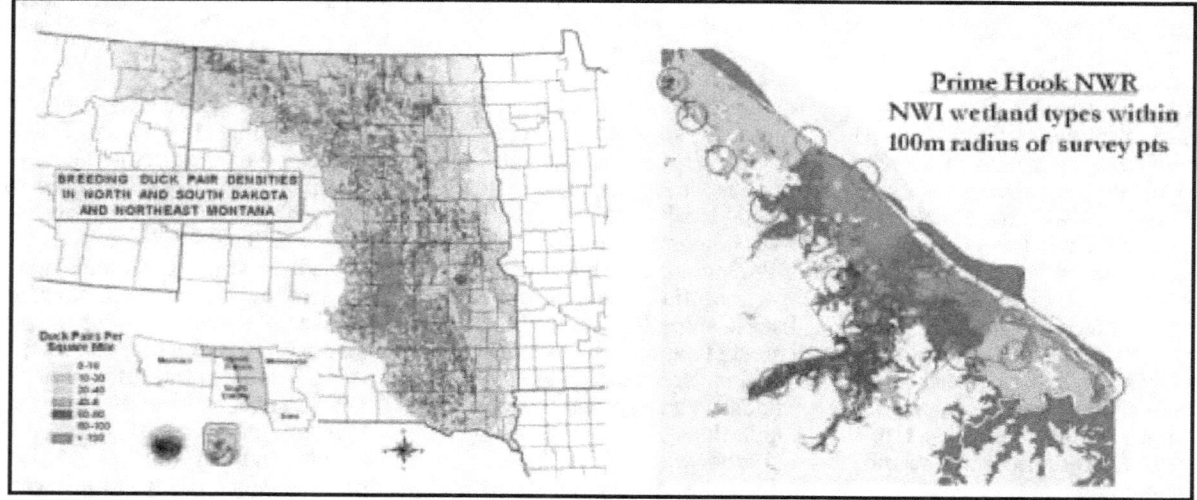

Figure 13. NWI data are used in conducting migratory bird surveys to identify bird density in various habitats: breeding pairs in the Prairie Potholes Region (left) and marsh bird habitat preferences as part of a nationwide survey (right).

for use in watershed condition assessments.

Riparian Habitat Classification and Mapping. In the regions where evaporation exceeds precipitation, riparian habitats are as critical for wildlife as wetlands are in the more humid regions. As much as 80 percent of wildlife species in these regions depend on riparian habitats. Such habitats are important migration corridors. The condition of riparian habitats is also important for maintaining healthy aquatic systems. Given these well-recognized values, the NWI felt it would be beneficial to include these habitats in its inventory in Regions 1, 2, 6, and 8. To standardize this mapping, the NWI developed a riparian classification system and mapping conventions (U.S. Fish and Wildlife Service 1997). This classification has been used in combination with the FWS's wetland classification system to produce NWI maps showing both riparian areas and wetlands in the arid regions of the country (Figure 14).

Enhanced NWI Data for Landscape-level Wetland Characterizations and Functional Assessments. In the 1970s and 1980s, the basic need for wetland data was inventory-based, that is, knowing where wetlands were on the landscape and how they differed in terms of vegetation type and hydrology. With strengthened wetland regulations since the late 1980s and early 1990s, another need has surfaced - wetland functional assessment. As techniques were being developed for on-the-ground assessment of wetland functions, the NWI sought ways to enhance its inventory so that landscape-level assessments of wetland functions could be derived from its database. To accomplish this, hydrogeomorphic-type descriptors were created to describe landscape position (i.e., the relationship between a wetland and a waterbody if present), landform (the shape or physical form of a wetland), and water flow path (the directional flow of water). In addition, other descriptors were formulated to better address the diversity of waterbodies, especially for ponds, since every wetland trend study

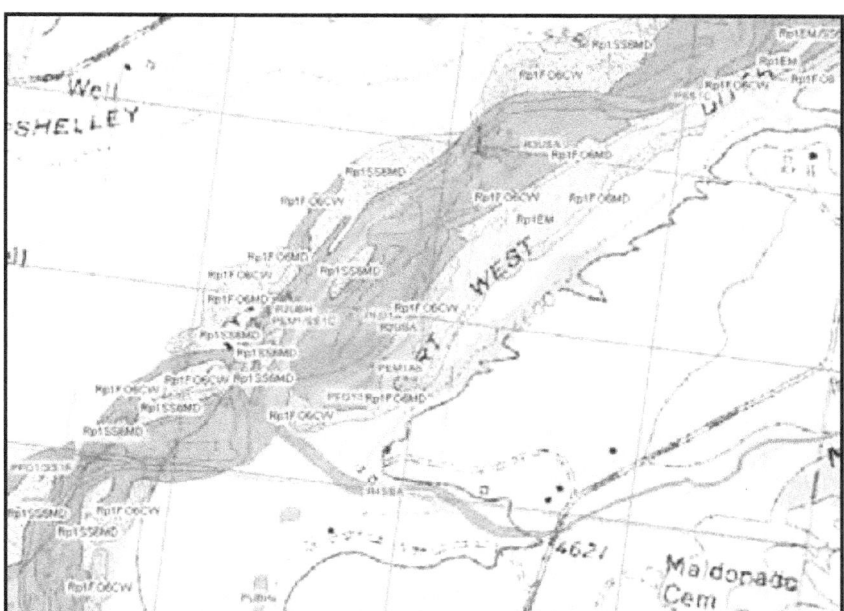
Figure 14. Portion of an NWI map showing wetlands and riparian habitats.

showed an increase in pond acreage while vegetated wetlands declined. Collectively these descriptors are referred to as LLWW descriptors (landscape position, landform, water flow path, and waterbody type; Tiner 2003). Applying these descriptors to the NWI database significantly increases the functionality of the database. The NWI has worked with wetland specialists in the Northeast to develop correlations between wetland functions and the wetland characteristics recorded in the enhanced NWI database (Tiner 2003b). The NWI has used these techniques to produce watershed-based wetland characterizations and preliminary functional assessments for a number of watersheds in the Northeast (Figure 15) and is applying these procedures in pilot study areas across the Nation (e.g., Anchorage Alaska, California's Ventura River watershed, Corpus Christi area of Texas, South Carolina's Horry and Jasper Counties, the Mississippi Coast, and Wyoming's Shirley basin). The results of the pilot studies will be published in 2010. A few states are applying these attributes to their wetland data. Recently, the Federal Geographic Data Committee's federal wetland mapping standard includes a recommendation to add these descriptors to wetland inventories to increase the

functionality of the database. In FY2010, NWI will publish reports for wetlands in New Jersey, Rhode Island, Delaware, South Carolina, Mississippi, Texas, and other areas that include preliminary functional assessments.

Potential Wetland Restoration Site Mapping. For special projects, the NWI has inventoried potential wetland restoration sites (Figure 16). These sites include former wetlands that have been drained or filled but are still in a condition where restoration is possible (Type 1 restoration sites) and existing wetlands that have functions impaired by ditching, excavation, impoundment, or cultivation (farmed wetlands). The former sites are identified using soil maps and locating hydric soil areas that are not mapped as NWI wetlands and do not have any buildings or other structures built upon them. Type 1 sites are mostly cropland on hydric soils (effectively drained sites), but also may include former wetlands that have been used as dredge material disposal sites and other impoundments. These restoration site inventories are often part of watershed-based wetland inventories and functional assessments as the data used in these investigations make it easy to document potential wetland

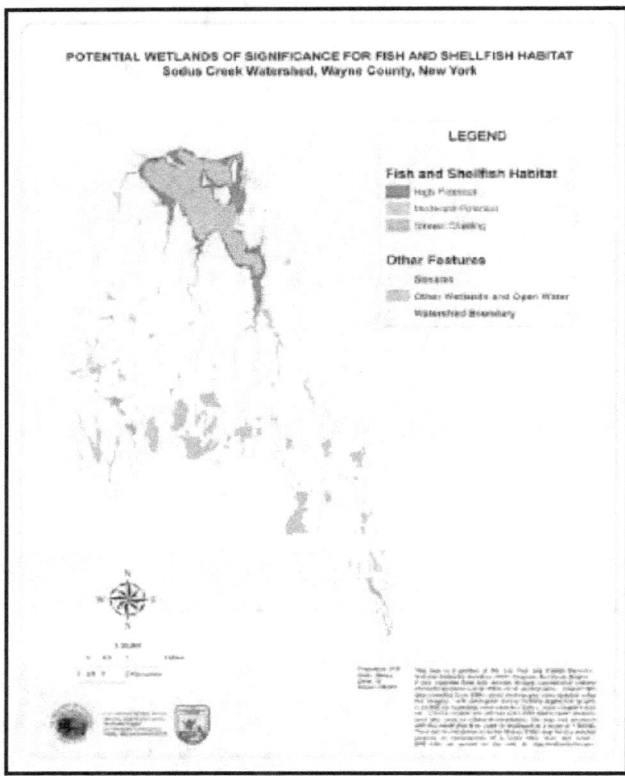

Figure 15. Example of a watershed map showing wetlands with potential for provision of fish and shellfish habitat.

dammed stream flowage, channelized stream flowage, wetland disturbance, and habitat fragmentation by roads. The last index - "composite natural habitat integrity index" – may be calculated in two ways: one is comprised of the weighted sum of the habitat extent indices minus the sum of the disturbance indices (weighted composite natural habitat integrity index), while the alternative is a simple sum of the extent indices minus the sum of the disturbance indices (simple summed composite natural habitat integrity index). These indices were intended to augment, not supplant, other more rigorous, fine-filter approaches for describing the ecological condition of watersheds and for examining relationships between human impacts and natural resources. NWI has applied the indices to special projects funded by the Service or state agencies interested in assessing the overall condition of natural habitat for individual watersheds (e.g., Tiner and Bergquist 2007). Region 3 has also applied these indices to their entire region to produce a map of watershed health (Figure 17). The State of Montana has adapted these techniques for assessing individual watersheds (e.g., Vance et al. 2009), while the Commonwealth of Virginia has used some of these indices in their watershed integrity model to report on the health of the state's watersheds (Ciminelli and Scrivani 2007).

restoration sites. In watershed assessments, it is also possible to identify sites for possible restoration of streamside vegetation.

Tool for Assessing Natural Habitat Integrity. The health of wetlands and waters is dependent on the condition of adjacent lands, with the condition of wetland and stream buffers being particularly important for wetland and aquatic wildlife. With the availability of land use/cover geospatial data, it is possible to integrate NWI data with such data to show and report on the condition of natural habitat surrounding these features and for watersheds as a whole. The NWI developed a set of "natural habitat integrity indices" that can be used for reporting on the condition of natural habitats for large geographic areas (Tiner 2004). Thirteen indices were created: seven addressing habitat extent (i.e., the amount of natural habitat occurring in the watershed and along wetlands and waterbodies), four dealing with habitat disturbances (emphasizing human-induced alterations to streams, wetlands, and terrestrial

habitats), and one composite index. The eight "natural" habitat extent indices are "natural" cover, river corridor integrity, stream corridor integrity, vegetated wetland buffer integrity, pond buffer integrity, lake buffer integrity, wetland extent, and standing waterbody extent. The four "habitat disturbance indices" involve

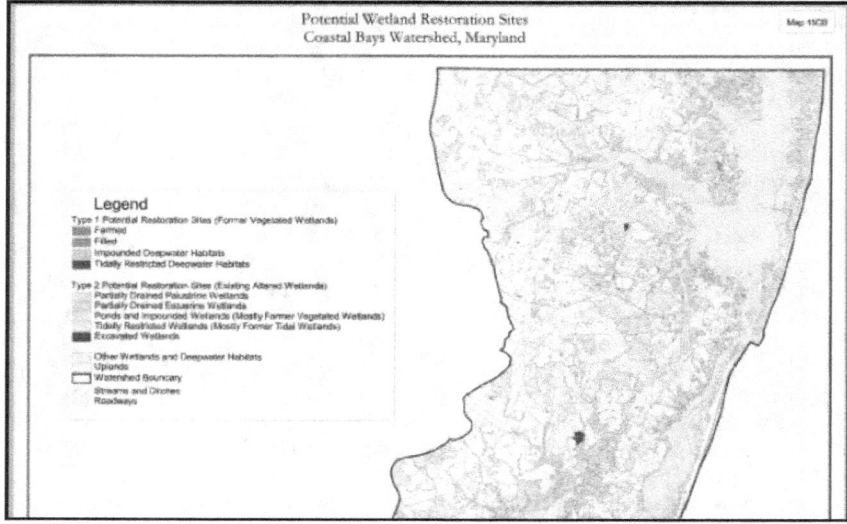

Figure 16. Portion of potential wetland restoration map for Maryland's Coastal Bays watershed.

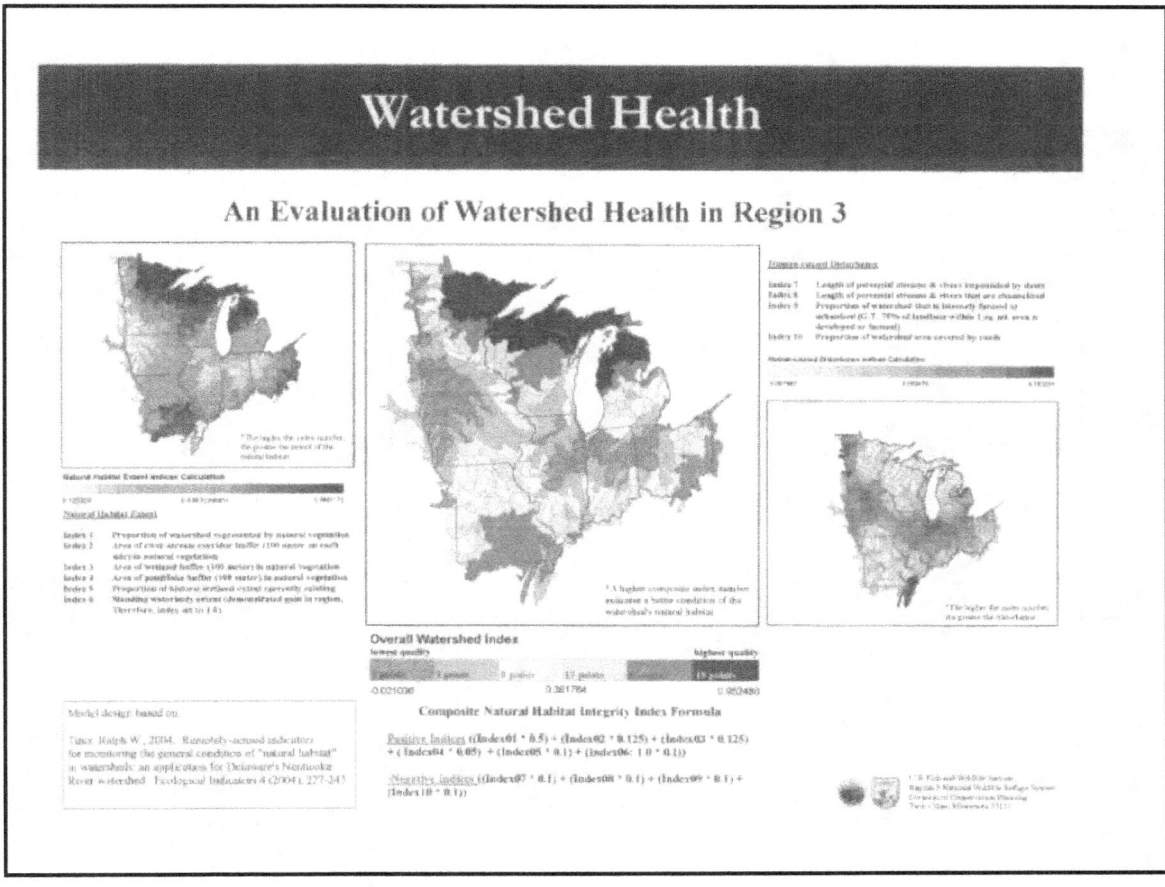

Figure 17. Region 3 poster detailing watershed health across the region based on application of natural habitat indices. (Note: This is the first version for the region.)

Regional Status of the NWI

Photo Credit: USFWS

Region 1/8: Pacific and Pacific Southwest
by Bill Kirchner
Regional Wetland Coordinator
USFWS, Region 1/8, Portland, OR

Current Mapping Status. Nearly all of the Region has been mapped with the only areas lacking NWI data being parts of Idaho, Nevada, and southern California (see status map below). California's Coast Range has 1970s-era NWI data in map form only, while the state's desert area in the southeast is the only area without NWI maps. For the five main islands of Hawaii, NWI data were derived from 1970s imagery, except for Oahu and Kauai which were updated using 2005 imagery. About 37 percent of Idaho has NWI data in digital form, and many areas have not been mapped. Most of Nevada's NWI digital data come from maps at the 1:250,000-scale. A few areas have more detailed data including Humbolt River corridor and associated drainages and lakes around Reno. NWI data for Oregon were derived from 1970s imagery along the coast and 1980s imagery for the majority of the state; the entire coast has been updated with 2005 data. Washington is completely mapped and digitized. Its 1,487 quads mostly reflect 1980s status, while areas in the northern Cascades and eastern basin represent 1970s status.

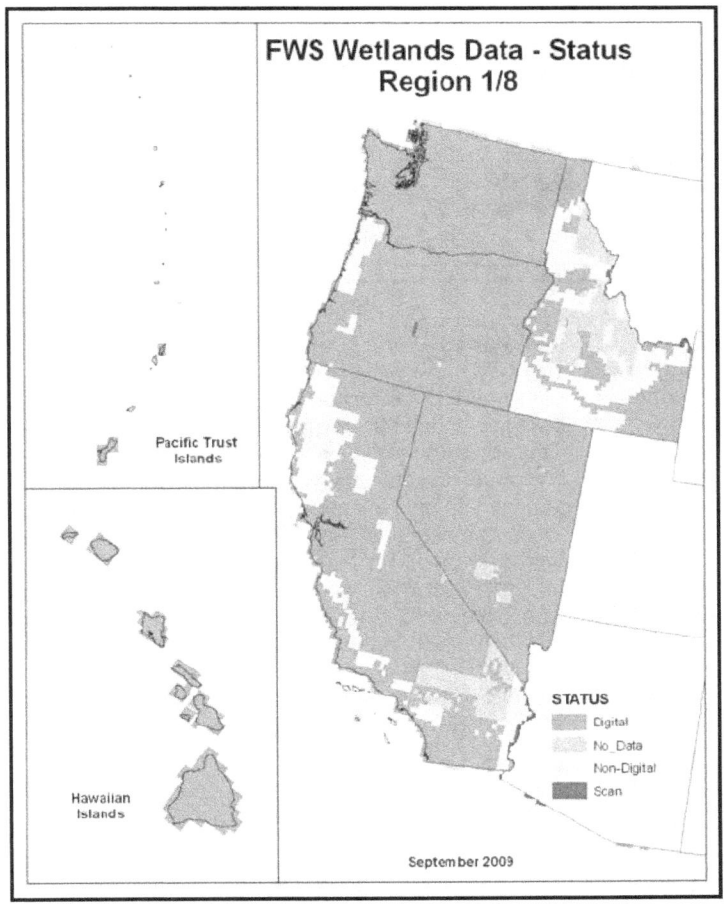

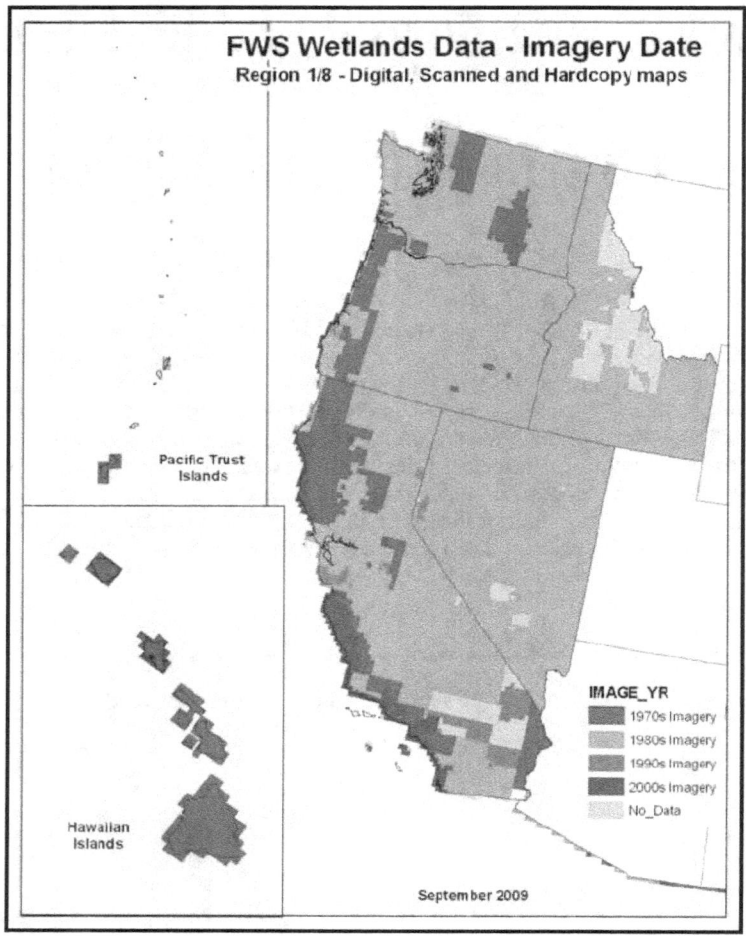

FWS Wetlands Data - Imagery Date
Region 1/8 - Digital, Scanned and Hardcopy maps

FY09 Mapping Activities. In California we continued to complete quads covering the Salinas River Valley. Eighteen quads were updated by the California State University, Monterey Bay. For the Hawaiian Islands, NWI data for the island of Kauai (12 quads) were updated. The Oregon Watershed Enhancement Board funded the digitizing of the remaining 748 NWI raster scans to bring the statewide NWI digital coverage to 100 percent: 703 quads representing 24.3 million acres worth of data were added to the wetlands master geospatial database this year.

Mapping in Progress for FY2010. A strategic refuge mapping initiative was started in 2007 to produce contemporary digital NWI data for more efficient project evaluation and assessment of impacts to species of concern at each refuge. In FY2010, work will continue on the following refuges: Julia Butler Hansen (WA),

Malheur (OR) and Humboldt Bay (CA). We will complete NWI mapping for California's Napa and Sonoma Valleys (a 17-quad update). The State of California is updating 193 quads in southern California and we will provide quality control. We are working with the Hoopa Valley Tribe (CA) on a wetlands inventory for their reservation where we provide training in wetland classification and mapping and will complete quality control to produce NWI-compliant data. We will provide quality assurance for the continued digitization of the Oregon maps.

FY09 Special Projects.

Support for National Wetlands Status and Trends Project. In 2009 and throughout 2010, Region 1 conducted and will pursue the completion of change analysis for all the national wetland status and trend plots in Region 1/8 states

as well as the plots in Utah and Montana. We will also conduct the review and analysis for the 290 new West Coast plots that are needed for EPA's 2011 wetland condition assessment report.

Field Office Support. The Region provided technical assistance to the Central Washington Field Office by completing NWI updates on a four-quad area in the Yakima River basin. The data are being used for cumulative impact analysis by the field office to determine the impacts of gravel mining on hydrology and wetland resources in the floodplain.

FY09 Coordination with Others. The R1/8 NWI is working with a number of agencies to carry out the mission of the NWI; these agencies have been listed in the mapping status section above. We are also working with the Idaho Fish and Game to digitize existing maps in the Clearwater River Basin. In

FY2010 we plan to work with the State of California in conducting for a statewide trend analysis.

FY09 Presentations. 1) "Assessment of Wetland Functions Using Enhanced National Wetlands Inventory Data: Ventura River Watershed (California) and Nanticoke River Watershed (Maryland and Delaware)" at Association of State Wetland Managers Conference (October 2008), Portland, OR.; 2) "Sea Level Affecting Marsh Model (SLAMM)" at Oregon State FWS Office (July 2009), Portland , OR.

FY09 Other Activities. R1/8 NWI provides direction and leadership for updating the "National List of Plants that Occur in Wetlands." The Regional Coordinator continues to work with the Corps of Engineers, Natural Resource Conservation Service, and the Environmental Protection Agency on this effort that should produce a new national wetland plant list for public review and comment in 2010. We also provide technical support to the State of California in the development of a statewide wetland monitoring program. To date a technical definition of "wetlands" and a draft rapid assessment method to evaluate wetland functions have been produced; for 2010 development of the monitoring program will continue and we will provide technical support on a planned statewide status and trend study.

Regional Applications of NWI Data. The following are some examples of uses of NWI data.

Identification of Internationally Important Wetlands. With the completion of the update for Kauai, the Region is working with the Field Office and the State of Hawaii to have the Alakai Swamp, a montane wet forest, designated as a World Wetland Ramsar Site.

Local Wetland Protection. The City of Seattle has a local wetland ordinance that is used to protect wetland resources. The Region provided updated NWI data to the City for use by their Planning Department in monitoring and tracking of wetland restoration, loss, and mitigation of unavoidable impacts.

Endangered or Rare Species Habitat Conservation. NWI data are used to map critical habitat of the endangered tidewater goby *(Eucyclogobius newberryi)* and in the development of the recovery plan and designation of critical habitat for this species.

Contaminant Effects on Wetland Wildlife. NWI data were used to map feeding habitat for the western tundra swan *(Cygnus columbianus)* in Idaho's Coeur d'Alene Basin. The data were then used to calculate the injury to this species from the release of lead into the feeding habitat and damages associated with a natural resource damage and assessment case. NWI data for Lake Roosevelt (WA) are being used to develop a wetland sampling plan to assess contaminant levels and trust resource injuries that may be occurring from the release of hazardous materials into the lake. The area is under investigation by the Service and the EPA.

Wildlife Refuge Planning and Conservation. NWI digital data are used for refuge planning efforts (e.g., Comprehensive Conservation Plans) across the Region. In particular, coastal refuges are using NWI data in models that predict the effect of various sea-level rise scenarios on tidal marshes and adjacent lowlands (i.e., SLAMM). SLAMM (Sea Level Affecting Marshes Model) has been applied to several refuges and the entire Puget Sound estuary. Region 1 procured a viewer from Image Matters to visually illustrate habitat changes in the Puget Sound area due to sea-level rise. The viewer was demonstrated at the 2008 Wetland and Global Climate Change conference hosted by the Association of State Wetland Managers and the Pacific Northwest Chapter of the Society of Wetland Scientists.

Regional Wetland Publications. The following is a list of some of the more significant wetland publications produced by the Region's NWI program. Other publications may be present; contact the Regional Coordinator for a complete listing.

Kirchner, W.N., J. Miner, and R. Griffin. 2008. Redwood National Park Wetlands and Waters: Results of the National Wetland Inventory. U.S. Fish and Wildlife Service, Pacific Region, Portland, OR.

Kirchner, W.N., J. Miner, and R. Griffin. 2008. Whiskeytown National Recreation Area Wetlands and Waters: Results of the National Wetland Inventory. U.S. Fish and Wildlife Service, Pacific Region, Portland, OR.

Kirchner, W.N., J. Miner, and R. Griffin. 2008. Florrisant National Park Wetlands and Waters: Results of the National Wetland Inventory. U.S. Fish and Wildlife Service, Pacific Region, Portland, OR. U.S. Fish and Wildlife Service, Pacific Region, Portland, OR.

Kirchner, W.N., J. Miner, and R. Griffin. 2008. Oregon Caves National Park Wetlands and Waters: Results of the National Wetland Inventory. U.S. Fish and Wildlife Service, Pacific Region, Portland, OR.

Region 2: Southwest
by Jim Dick
Regional Wetland Coordinator
USFWS, Region 2, Albuquerque, NM

Current Mapping Status. NWI data are available for nearly the entire Region, except for a few areas in New Mexico and Texas. Most of these data are in map form only and not available in digital format for GIS and computer applications. Digital data are available for most of Oklahoma, coastal Texas, the Playa Region of Texas and New Mexico, some river corridors, and several other areas across the Region. Scans of NWI hardcopy maps have been produced for other areas so that NWI data can be viewed online via the Wetlands Mapper. *Note: The State of Texas maintains its own database of scanned NWI maps for the entire state. These data are not currently part of the National Dataset. For further information, please contact the Texas Natural Resources Information System (TNRIS).*

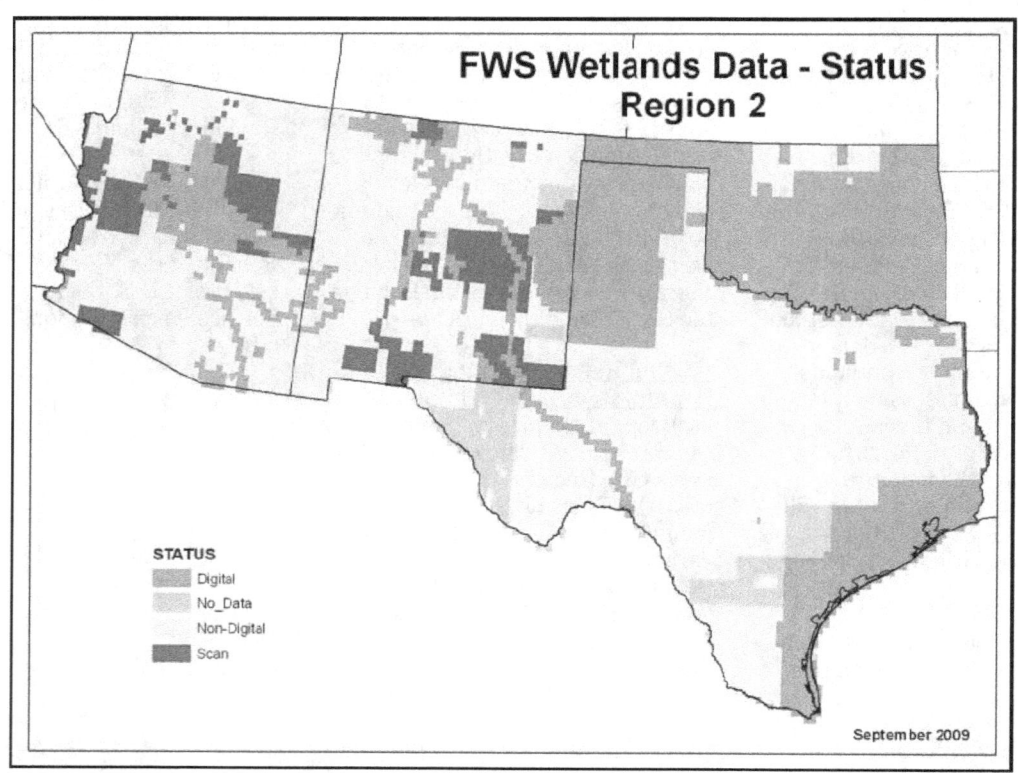

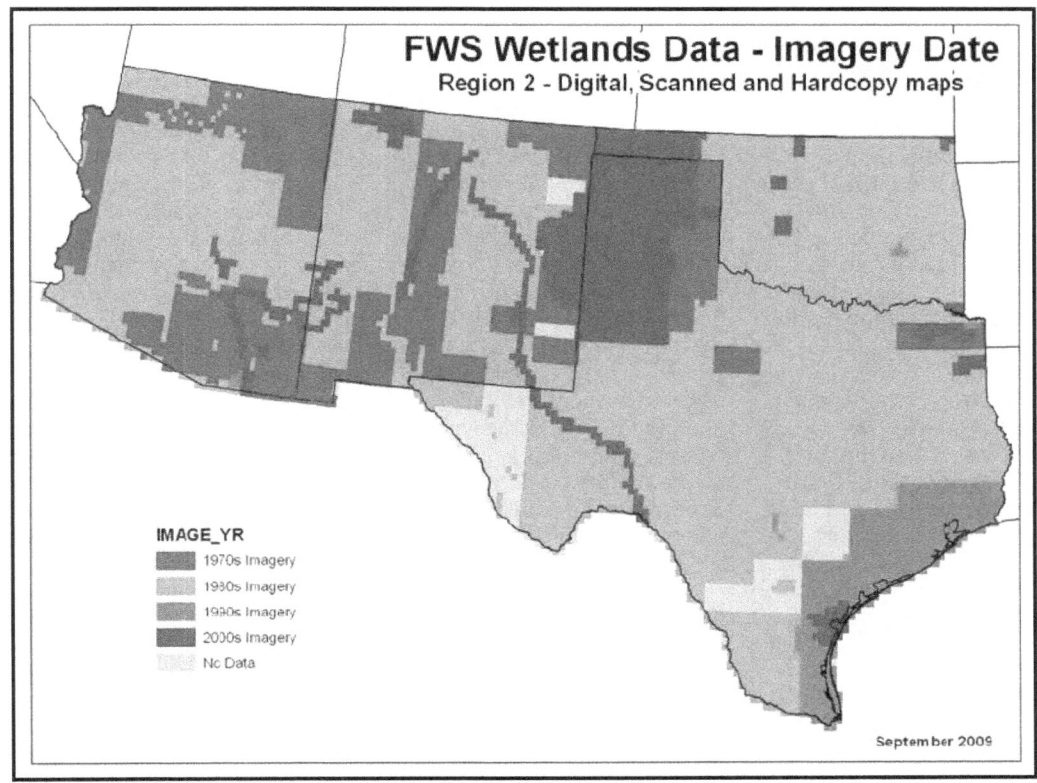

FY09 Mapping Activities. Work continued on updating critical areas of the Texas coast for the Gulf/Atlantic National Project. We initiated updated mapping for the area surrounding the Aransas National Wildlife Refuge, part of updating NWI data for coastal refuges along the Atlantic and Gulf coasts (FY2010). We are cooperating with state agencies and others to get NWI data digitized and entered into the wetlands master geospatial database. This year over 24 million acres of digitized NWI data were added the wetlands master geospatial database and Wetlands Mapper. The Oklahoma Conservation Commission, in conjunction with Oklahoma State University, digitized NWI data for almost 13 million acres (349 quads) of land in Oklahoma. The Commission has now acquired digital wetlands data for nearly 90% of the state. The Tennessee Valley Authority digitized NWI data for over 11 million acres (282 quads) covering U.S. Forest Service National Forests in Arizona and New Mexico.

Mapping in Progress for FY2010. An intraregional collaborative effort

(Regions 2, 4, and 5) has been initiated between NWI and the National Wildlife Refuge System to provide updated wetlands data for all refuges on the Atlantic and Gulf coasts. NWI data for Aransas and Laguna Atascosa NWRs will be updated. Other NWI-funded mapping includes Texas Playa Region (15 counties; 290 quads) and Arizona updates (Agua Fria watershed; 70 quads). The State of New Mexico will be updating NWI data for the Canadian River watershed and northeastern New Mexico (approx. 50 1:24K quads), while the Navajo Nation will be updating NWI data for about 400 quads. The State of Oklahoma is digitizing 190 existing NWI maps and the Tennessee Valley Authority is digitizing NWI maps for the Forest Service lands in Arizona and New Mexico (660 quads; 21 map scans).

FY09 Special Projects.

Support for National Wetlands Status and Trends Project. R2 NWI continues to provide support for the 2010 national wetlands status and trends study that is currently

underway: change analysis continues on the 293 four-square mile plots within the State of Texas with future work planned for Louisiana and New Mexico for FY2010.

FY09 Coordination with Others. The Regional Coordinator sits on the Service's Regional Climate Change implementation Team that is developing support documentation for the development of the Regional Geographic Framework upon which all climate change activities will be based. R2 NWI initiated an interagency agreement with the U.S. Geological Survey Texas Cooperative Fish & Wildlife Research Unit at Texas Tech University (USGS-TTU) to fund digital mapping and data analysis to evaluate the feasibility of developing ecological models to predict potential effects of climate change on the playa lakes of the Southern Great Plains. The Texas Tech Geography Department, Center for Geospatial Technology will complete the updated mapping for the Texas Panhandle. For this project, we trained ten students in wetland delineation and photo interpretation. We developed an interagency

17

agreement with the U.S. Geological Survey/ National Wetlands Research Center (Lafayette, LA) to fund the first phase of digital wetlands mapping on the south Texas coast and Laguna Atascosa National Wildlife Refuge. (Note: Both of these agreements tie into the Regional Climate Change Geographic Framework; the Texas Coast and the Southern Great Plains are the primary areas of interest for Region 2 for implementing Strategic Habitat Conservation (SHC) techniques related to evaluating the effects of climate change to species and their habitats. NWI is now tied into both of these areas through these USGS partnerships.) We provided training to the Navajo Nation to support their effort to update NWI for their entire Reservation (378 quads in NM, CO, UT, and AZ); we will also assist with data quality control, field surveys, and any other required functions needed to complete the project. R2 NWI provided guidance in project design and training in wetland classification and mapping to the University of Arizona for conducting a statewide NWI map updating project sponsored by the Arizona Department of Environmental Quality; we will also assist in field surveys and other ways to help complete this project. We worked with the State of New Mexico in drafting a proposal that included updating and enhancing NWI data for the Canadian River Watershed and Northeast New Mexico. The State's Surface Water Quality Bureau (SWQB) has received funding for this project through an EPA grant; work will be done in FY2010.

FY09 Presentations. 1) "Applying NWI Data to Landscape-level Resource Management" at Association of State Wetland Managers Annual Meeting (March 17, 2009), National Conservation Training Center, Shepherdstown, WV; 2) "Addressing Current Coastal Issues with NWI Data: Texas Coast" Southeastern Association of Fish & Wildlife Agencies (October 12, 2008), Corpus Christi, TX, and 3) "Addressing Current Coastal Issues with NWI Data: Texas Coast" at Texas State Trustee Meeting

(October 7, 2008) in Corpus Christi, TX.

FY09 Other Activities. Region 2's NWI Program has a unique role as the Riparian Data Steward for the country. This fiscal year, we updated the riparian data collection document: "A System for Mapping Riparian Areas in the Western United States (U.S. Fish and Wildlife Service 1997)." The document should be available to the public early next fiscal year. We also assisted in the development, editing and final review of the wetland data collection standards document – "Data Collection Requirements and Procedures for Mapping Wetland, Deepwater and Related Habitats of the United States" (Dahl et al. 2009).

Regional Applications of NWI Data. The following are some examples of uses of NWI data.

Identification of Restorable Playas. The Regional Environmental Contaminants Program; Natural Resource Damage Assessment (NRDA) has been using updated NWI digital data to identify playas in need of restoration in eastern New Mexico. This program is working with local landowners to restore these important wetland habitats by providing funding and ecological guidance. Some of the restoration/ improvements that are being applied include removing excavated ponds from within the playas, creating grass (native vegetation) buffers to limit sedimentation and ceasing agricultural practices in dry years. Playa lakes, in eastern New Mexico, are important feeding areas for migrating birds.

Development of Shoreline Management Plans. The Grand River Dam Authority (GRDA) is developing shoreline management plans for a series of large reservoirs in northeastern Oklahoma. Increasing pressures from development, both urban and agricultural, have been cutting into these vanishing wetland habitats. GRDA is using updated NWI digital data to identify wetlands associated with these reservoirs and to develop a plan to manage development along these lakes including preservation of

remaining bottomland habitats.

Endangered Species Conservation. The Endangered Species Program has been using digital NWI data on the Texas coast to aid in the designation of critical habitat for the wintering population of the threatened piping plover (Charadrius melodus). By referring to certain Cowardin codes in the NWI database, ES biologists are able to construct more accurate maps that identify critical habitat areas. The NWI completed wetlands and riparian habitat mapping and a wetland assessment report assessing changes and damages to wetland/riparian vegetative communities along a stretch of the Gila River as a result of a major flood in February of 2005. This stretch of river is considered a key area for potential southwestern willow flycatcher (Empidonax traillii extimus) habitat restoration activities of the Service and other organizations. This flycatcher nests in fairly dense riparian tree and shrub communities, usually associated with rivers, swamps, and other wetlands, mostly in forested and scrub/shrub wetlands. Having the remaining riparian habitats mapped in digital format allows GIS analysis for planning habitat re-establishment or enhancement. Once recovery projects are completed, NWI data will be used to monitoring accomplishments to see if desired results are achieved and maintained over the time period required to meet the recovery goal to increase or improve occupied, suitable, and potential breeding habitat. The greatest threat facing the threatened Chiricahua leopard frog (Rana chiricahuensis) is the highly-invasive eastern bullfrog (Rana catesbeiana). Using digital maps that were prepared in a limited pilot project by the National Wetlands Inventory covering 70 thousand acres, recovery efforts are underway to identify remote wetlands that can have bullfrogs removed and that could resist re-colonization. Wetlands geospatial data used in a GIS (geographic information system) analysis will generate distances between sites, locate unknown wetlands for possible re-introduction, and identify possible sites for future restoration. These digital maps also cover about 20% of the current habitat of the endangered Sonora tiger salamander *(Ambystoma tigrinum stebbinsi)*, also vulnerable to bullfrogs and other invasive species, and will be used to aid in similar recovery efforts. These maps were produced at a much finer scale than the regular NWI maps in order to locate smaller-sized wetlands, mostly stock ponds - the current primary habitat for both species.

Identification of Internationally Important Wetlands. The Service's New Mexico Ecological Services Field Office, BLM, and the State of New Mexico are using NWI digital data along the Pecos River in southeastern New Mexico in an attempt to designate a rare (for the arid west) artesian outflow wetland complex as a World Wetland Ramsar Site. A Ramsar Wetland nomination could include the unique saline wetlands, saltgrass wet meadows, saltgrass marshes, iodine bush flats, cattail and bulrush marshes, playas, sinkhole lakes, and wetland channels that are found on the public lands

of the Bitter Lake National Wildlife Refuge, the Bottomless Lakes State Park and the Bureau of Land Management Overflow Wetlands Area of Critical Environmental Concern. These "Roswell artesian wetlands" have a unique hydrology and are known to play a vital role in providing important feeding areas and resting habitat for more than 20,000 migratory birds. Several unique plants and animals, such as Pecos sunflower *(Helianthus paradoxus)*, Wright's marsh thistle *(Cirsium wrightii)*, Pecos pupfish *(Cyprinodon pecosensis)*, Mexican tetra *(Astyanax mexicanus)*, arid land ribbon snake *(Thamnophis proximus diabolicus)*, Blanchard's cricket frog *(Acris crepitans blanchardi)*, least shrew *(Cryptotis parva)*, and Roswell springsnail *(Pyrgulopsis roswellensis)* as well as over 90 species of dragonflies and damselflies are also found in these unique wetland habitats.

Regional Wetland Publications.
The following is a list of wetland publications produced by or with the assistance of the Region's NWI program.

Dick, J. A. and R.B. McHale. 2007. Wetland and Riparian Habitats of the Playa Lakes Region: Status Report, 2006-2007. U.S. Fish and Wildlife Service, Southwest Region, Albuquerque, NM.

Dick, J. A. and R.B. McHale. 2006. Monitoring Changes to Wetland and Riparian Vegetation Resulting from the February 13th, 2005 Flood Event, Upper Gila River, Arizona. U.S. Fish and Wildlife Service, Southwest Region, Albuquerque, NM.

Moulton, D.W., T.E. Dahl, and D.M. Dall. 1997. Texas Coastal Wetlands: Status and Trends, Mid-1950s to Early 1990s. U.S. Department of the Interior, Fish and Wildlife Service, Southwestern Region, Albuquerque, NM. 32 pp.

Region 3: Great Lakes/Big Rivers
by Brian Huberty
Regional Wetland Coordinator
USFWS, Region 3, Ft Snelling, MN

Current Mapping Status. Nearly all of the Region has been mapped and a significant number of areas have been updated (at least once). Iowa is approaching completion and the Wisconsin Wetland Inventory data has been converted to NWI types and is entered in wetlands master geospatial database. Ducks Unlimited has finished digitizing and updating the northern half of Ohio as well as parts of Illinois, Indiana, and Michigan. The State of Minnesota is finishing the evaluation of NWI updating methodologies and plans to begin updating in 2010.

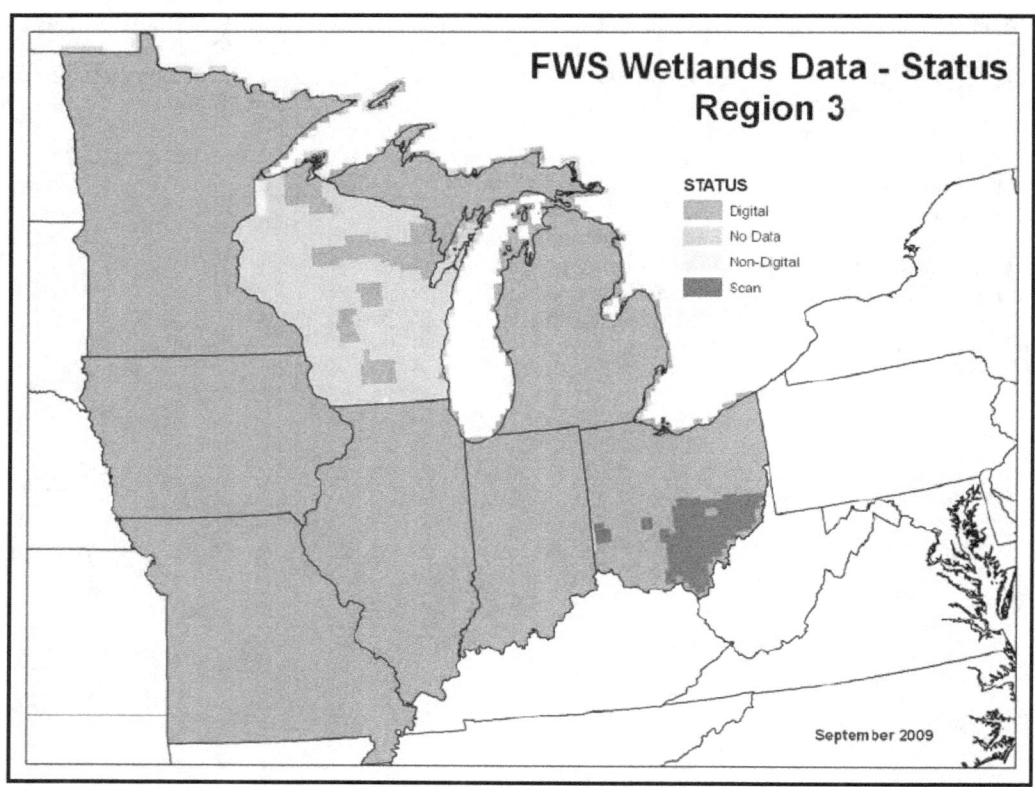

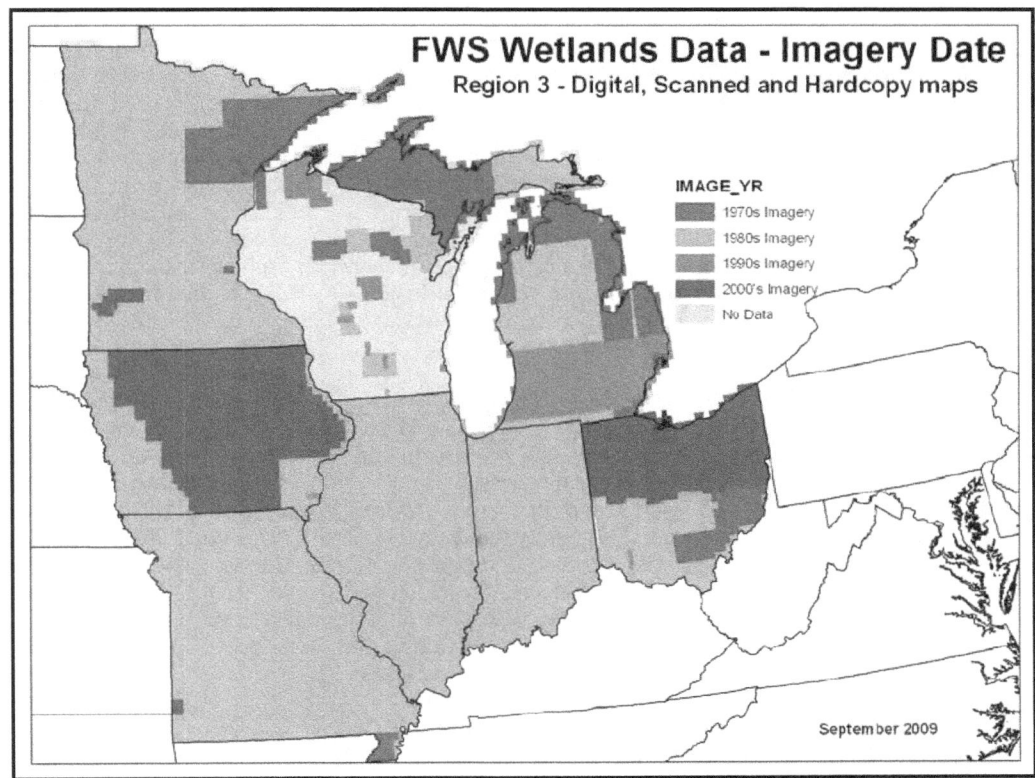

FY09 Mapping Activities. During this FY, the NWI Program converted Wisconsin wetland inventory data to NWI types so the data could be added to the national database. Contributed NWI data are coming from Ducks Unlimited who are mapping wetlands in Illinois, Ohio, and Michigan (see figure below – purple areas = completed; blue areas = in progress).

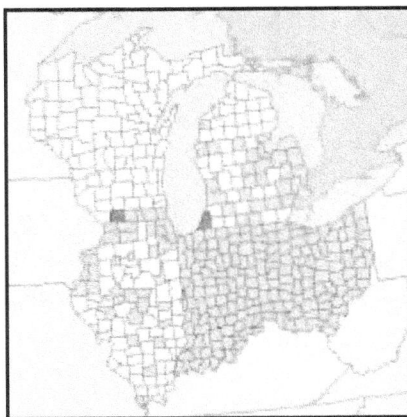

St Mary's University (WI) produced updated NWI data for a British Petroleum (BP) pipeline corridor (work funded entirely by BP).

Mapping in Progress for FY2010. NWI funding for mapping is undetermined at this time. The State of Minnesota plans to begin updating NWI data in 2010, while the State of Iowa will continue their efforts to update NWI.

FY09 Special Projects.

Restoration of Great Lakes Wetlands. R3 NWI is working with EPA on a Great Lakes Restoration Initiative to help restore the wetlands and other habitat for the Great Lakes; a proposal has been submitted that includes wetland mapping and imagery acquisition.

Minnesota Wetland Status and Trends. We are also working with: the State of Minnesota DNR on their statewide NWI update and upgrade program and the Minnesota Pollution Control Agency on their wetlands status and trends project.

Remote Sensing Applications for Detecting Common Reed. We are working with Michigan Tech University on a project investigating the application of satellite radar for mapping common reed (*Phragmites australis*) – an invasive species

threatening many wetlands across the country.

FY09 Presentations. R3 NWI worked with USGS Great Lakes Science Center to organize and lead a day-long symposium on Wetland Remote Sensing and Mapping at the Society for Wetland Scientists Annual Meeting (June 23, 2009), Madison, WI; presented "Remote Sensing Technologies Overview for Mapping and Monitoring Wetlands" at this meeting. Also presented "Remote Sensing Technologies Overview for Lake Michigan" at the 2009 Lake Michigan: State of the Lake Conference (September 29, 2009), Milwaukee, WI.

FY09 Coordination with Others. R3 NWI has cooperative agreements with: 1) Ducks Unlimited for helping update NWI, 2) Michigan Tech University for investigating the use of radar imaging for wetland extent and invasive species mapping, 3) the University of Minnesota for evaluating wetland mapping methodologies, and 4) St. Mary's University for updating Iowa's NWI maps and BP pipeline corridors. We are also working with EPA and others on the Great Lake

Restoration Initiative by developing project proposals to improve the wetlands and habitats within the Great Lakes watershed.

Regional Applications of NWI Data. The following are some examples of uses of NWI data.

Wetland Restoration, Creation, and Enhancement Planning. The Ducks Unlimited (DU) Great Lakes/Atlantic Region Office is not only a valued partner for help producing updated NWI maps but is also a prime user of NWI data. Their field biologists regularly use updated NWI maps to help plan wetland restoration, creation and enhancement projects out in the field. DU also uses NWI data with their Habitat Evaluation Network (HEN) model to plan and target habitat conservation in the Great Lakes states. HEN allows both DU and its partners to enhance and refine wetland and upland habitat programs for breeding mallards under the North American Waterfowl Management Plan and the Upper Mississippi/Great Lakes Joint Venture.

Energy Development Planning. WindLogics, a leading provider of wind knowledge for utility-scale project development and grid integration, is using NWI mapping data into their discovery study programs to assist landowners and developers with optimum wind farm site locations with minimal environmental impacts on wetlands. The company is also planning on incorporating other Service habitat products as they become available to help minimize environmental impacts with wind energy development projects.

Transportation Assistance. Primordial, an off-road navigation software development company, has developed "Ground Guidance" software which provides for an optimal route location through off-road terrain. They are using NWI maps in their navigation system to help refine routes to avoid wetland areas, thereby helping reduce the environmental impact of off-road vehicles. This software has both civilian and military applications.

Wetland Monitoring Design. The Iowa Department of Natural Resources used updated NWI data to randomly select sites for monitoring the condition of wetlands across the state. Semipermanently and permanently flooded potholes on public or private lands were selected for study. Chemical, physical, and biological parameters are being monitored to determine the ecological condition of Iowa's remaining wetlands.

Endangered or Rare Species Habitat Conservation. The Missouri Field Office uses NWI to help find additional occurrences of Hine's emerald dragonfly *(Somatochlora hineana)* - the only federally listed dragonfly protected under the Endangered Species Act. Part of the recovery plan was to conduct surveys in appropriate wetland habitat, mostly small fens crawfish burrows. Areas for surveys include states where the species currently exists, states where it existed historically, and neighboring states, 24 in total. At the end of the 2004 survey in Missouri, it was generally understood that all known high-quality fens had been searched and that it was unlikely additional population sites would be discovered. However in 2005, using NWI data for a 10-county area, the Columbia Missouri Field Office (CMFO) began looking for unknown fens. With partner Missouri Department of Conservation running a GIS analysis looking at NWI code PEMB (palustrine emergent wetland with saturated water regime), the CMFO was able to identify numerous potential sites with appropriate habitat that were unknown to conservation agencies in the state. As a result of this study, all researchers and enthusiasts in Missouri were convinced that using NWI digital maps data to identify new potential habitat in Missouri and other states would be a major contributing factor in expanding the knowledge and known distribution of the Hine's emerald dragonfly. To date, the Service has surveyed about 150 fens in Missouri and the number of known populations of dragonfly has increased from 3 to 27 sites. Once surveying is complete, the next step is to use the NWI data to

locate possible sites for restoration or for introduction of the species. These actions will enable the Service to meet the minimum number of individuals required in this population segment for downlisting the species from Endangered to Threatened and eventually for recovery and delisting. This step will be further facilitated once wetlands digital data in states with existing populations and the remainder of the 24 states of interest are updated from the mostly 1980s-era maps to the current era using finer imagery and more modern mapping techniques and standards. Two scientific papers have been written on this application of NWI (McKenzie 2005, 2005/6). Currently, the Service is using NWI data to identify potential whopping crane habitat.

Region 4: Southeast
by John Swords
Regional Wetland Coordinator
USFWS, Region 4, Atlanta, GA

Current Mapping Status. Seventy-eight percent of the Region has NWI data in digital format, yet most of that data reflects early 1980s conditions. Hardcopy maps or interpreted imagery (pen and ink-marked mylar overlays of aerial photographs) are the only available NWI product for much of Arkansas, Louisiana, and Mississippi. Conversion to digital data would require considerable effort and additional funding and besides, the data are from the 1970s and 1980s. Unfortunately, for most of the Southeast, the NWI data are now over 20 years old. As the age of the NWI data increases, the value of the data decreases. With rapid development in some areas (especially along the coast and in metropolitan areas), the existing NWI data are more of a historic representation of wetlands that once covered the region rather than a current account of wetlands. NWI are in dire need of updating. Consequently, the Region is reaching out for support from other federal and state agencies to accomplish this.

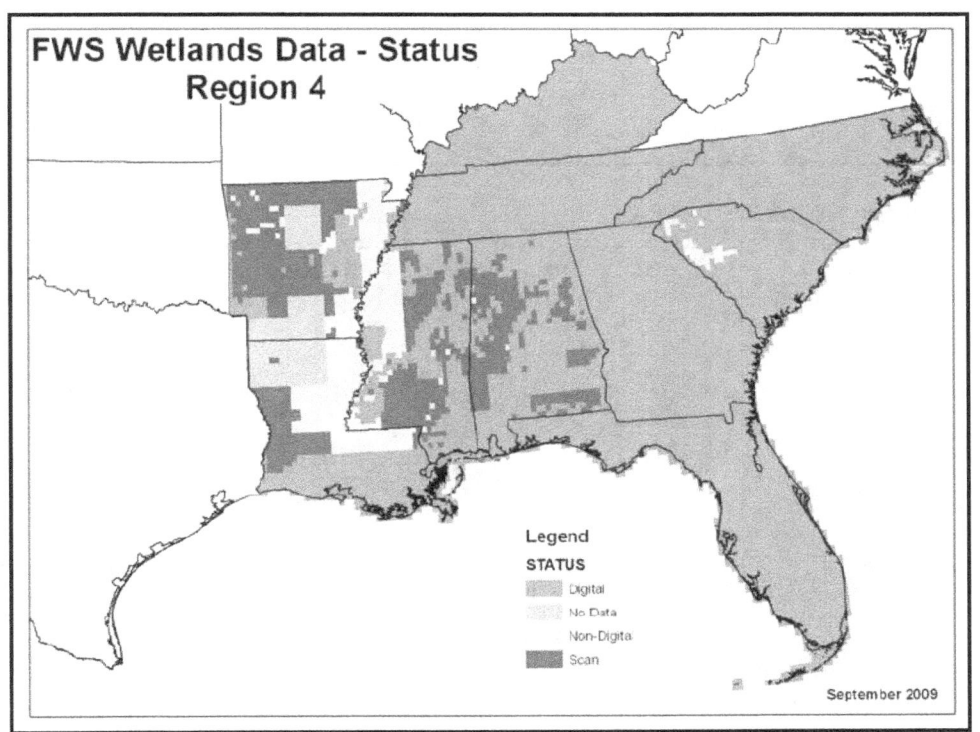

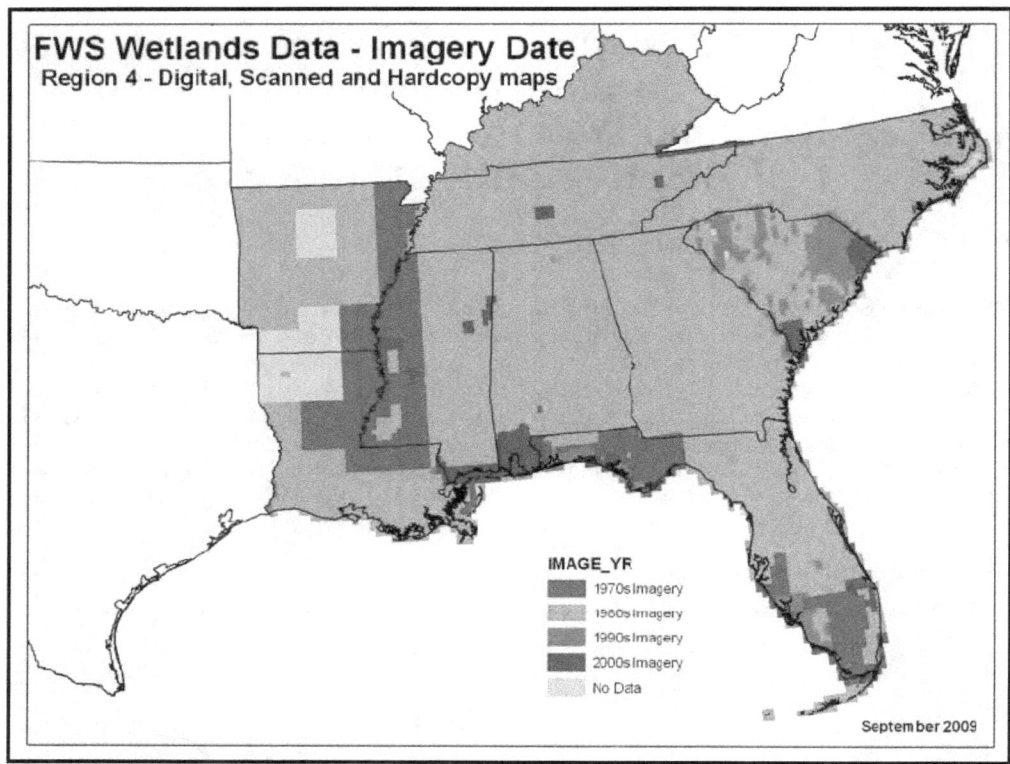

FWS Wetlands Data - Imagery Date
Region 4 - Digital, Scanned and Hardcopy maps

IMAGE_YR
- 1970s Imagery
- 1980s Imagery
- 1990s Imagery
- 2000s Imagery
- No Data

September 2009

FY09 Mapping Activities. NWI-funded projects completed and submitted to the NWI wetlands master geospatial database include coastal Mississippi quads (37), Tennessee Valley Authority climate change quads (12), and U.S. Virgin Islands updated quads (12) that incorporated lidar data that was contributed by the U.S. Virgin Islands Territorial Agencies. A GIS-conversion process transformed wetland data from Florida's land use/cover inventory into NWI data for nineteen 1:24K quads that included Archie Carr and Pelican Island National Wildlife Refuges. Also added to the wetlands master geospatial database were contributed data from the U.S. Geological Survey's Wetlands Research Center (Lafayette, LA) for Mobile Bay and Baldwin County (updated NWI data for 65 quads along the Alabama coast).

Mapping In Progress for FY2010. A major NWI initiative commenced in FY09 that will provide updated wetlands data for coastal National Wildlife Refuges. NWI data for the following refuges are being updated: Region 4 work will include the following thirty Refuges:

Alligator River (NC), Bayou Sauvage (LA), Big Branch Marsh (LA), Breton (LA), Buck Island (VI), Caloosahatchee (FL), Cape Romain (SC), Cedar Keys (FL), Cedar Island (NC), Chassahowitzka (FL), Crocodile Lake (FL), Currituck (NC), Delta (LA), Egmont Key (FL), Great White Heron (FL), Hobe Sound (FL), Key West (FL), Lower Suwannee (FL), Mackay Island (NC), Mattamuskett (NC), Merritt Island (FL), National Key Deer (FL), Passage Key (FL), Pea Island (NC), Pinellas (FL), Pocosin Lakes (NC), Roanoke River (NC), St. Marks (FL), Swanquarter (NC), and Ten Thousand Islands (FL). Additional ongoing projects include updates in Western Tennessee, Cape Canaveral Air Force Base (FL), and contributed data for coastal Georgia from the State of Georgia.

FY09 Special Projects.

Support for National Wetlands Status and Trends Project. R4NWI continues to provide support for the 2010 national wetlands status and trends study that is currently underway: change analysis continues on 130 four-square mile plots in South Carolina and Florida.

FY09 Presentations. "Enhancing NWI Data for Wetland Function and Natural Habitat Integrity Assessments" presentation at regional symposium – "Regional and Local Integration of GIS Technology," St Thomas, VI (November 20, 2008) and at St John's Water Management District - Palatka, FL (March 2009).

FY09 Coordination with Others. Ongoing work with Georgia DNR (EPA funded) to complete NWI data for 73 quads along the coast continues to move forward. R4 NWI is assisting with quality control to ensure that products meet NWI standards. Seeing the success of NWI's conversion of existing wetland data from Florida's land use/cover inventory to NWI types, the St. John's Water Management District is planning to conduct a pilot project applying the same techniques to convert their wetland data base to NWI types. In Puerto Rico, the Department of Natural Resources, Marine Resources and the Fisheries and Wildlife Bureau is in the process of identifying wetland priorities and needs. This action will aid in the pursuit of funding to get updated NWI information. Additionally, funding was also received from U.S. Army Corps of Engineers to update the NWI maps at Cape Canaveral Air Force Base (FL). R4 NWI has met with representatives from natural resource agencies from the Commonwealth of Puerto Rico, South Carolina, and Kentucky to discuss the value of updating and enhancing NWI data and have encouraged them to pursue EPA funds for wetlands mapping and assessments.

Regional Applications of NWI Data.
The following are some examples of uses of NWI data.

<u>Local Planning.</u> In Georgia NWI data is used for local comprehensive and ordinance plans, State Natural Heritage Inventory and addressing land conservation priorities.

<u>Data for Statewide GIS, Regional and Local Planning.</u> In South Carolina the NWI data is downloaded by South Carolina Departments of Health and Environmental Control, Commerce, Transportation (the State DOT), Parks, Recreation and Tourism, Forestry as well as every county and municipal government agency in the state that has a GIS program. South Carolina is planning on using NWI data to support various climate change modeling initiatives.

Comment: For most of the Region, NWI data are too old to be of value for most planning efforts, especially in the coastal zone where much development has occurred since the 1980s.

Regional Wetland Publications.
The following is a list of wetland publications produced by or with the assistance of the Region's NWI program.

Dahl, T.E. 1999 South Carolina's Wetlands – Status and Trends 1982-1989. U. S. Fish and Wildlife Service, Southeast Region, Atlanta, GA. 58 pp.

Dahl, T.E. 2005 Florida's Wetlands: An Update on Status and Trends 1985-1996. U.S. Fish and Wildlife Service, Southeast Region, Atlanta, GA. 80 pp.

Dahl, T.E., J. Swords, and M.T. Bergeson. 2009 Wetland Inventory of the Yazoo Backwater Area, Mississippi – Wetland Status and Potential Changes Based on an Updated Inventory Using Remotely Sensed Imagery. U.S. Fish and Wildlife Service, Division of Habitat and Resource Conservation, Washington, DC. 30 pp.

Frayer, W.E. and J.M. Hefner. Florida Wetlands: Status and Trends 1970s to 1980s. U.S. Fish and

Wildlife Service, Southeast Region, Atlanta, GA. 31 pp.

Hefner, J.M., B.O. Wilen, T.E. Dahl, and W.E. Frayer. 1994. Southeast Wetlands: Status and Trends, Mid-1970s to Mid-1980s. U.S. Department of the Interior, Fish and Wildlife Service, Atlanta, GA. 32 pp.

Region 5: Northeast
by Ralph Tiner
Regional Wetland Coordinator
USFWS, Region 5, Hadley, MA

Current Mapping Status. Nearly all of the Region has been mapped and a significant number of areas have been updated (at least once). Only the Adirondack region and a few small areas in New York have not been mapped. Updated NWI data based on 1990s or 2000s imagery are available for New Jersey, Rhode Island, much of the Maine and Massachusetts coasts, parts of western Vermont, Long Island (NY), Pennsylvania's Poconos Region, part of northeastern Maryland, the lower Delmarva Peninsula, and much of eastern and southwestern Virginia.

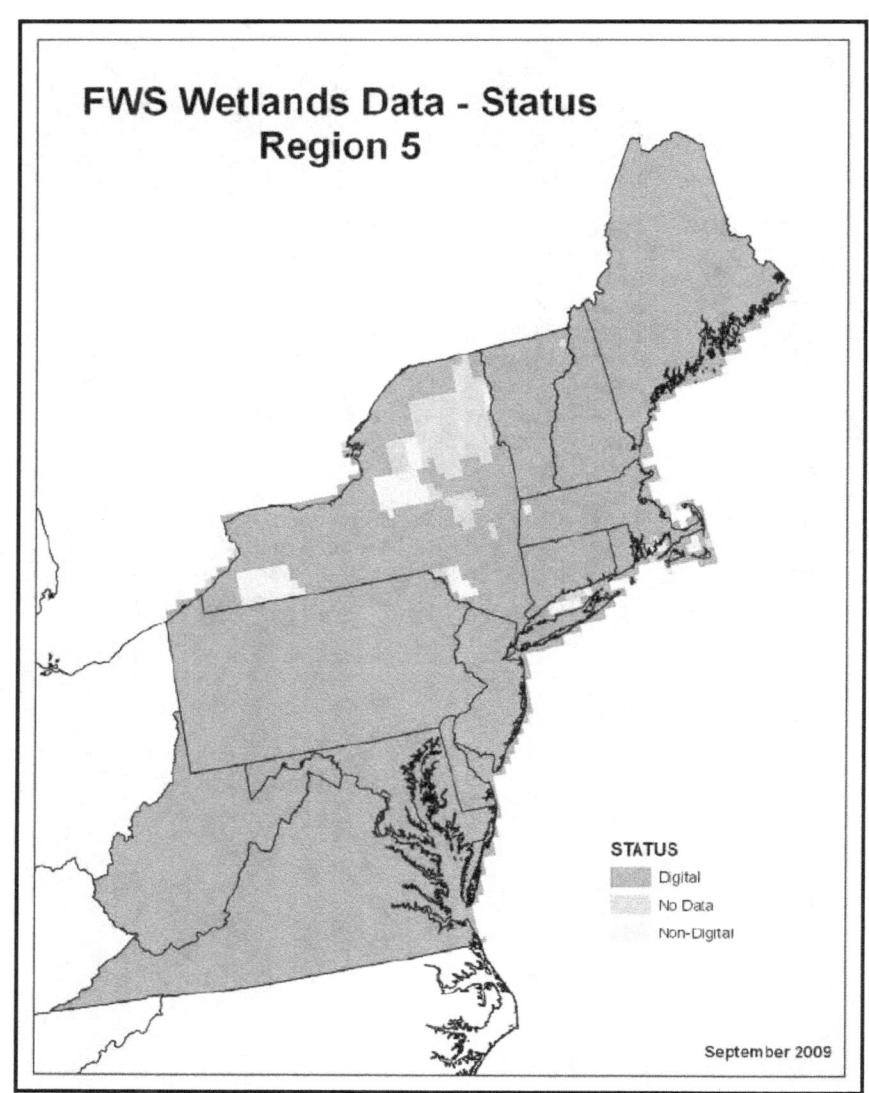

FWS Wetlands Data - Status
Region 5

STATUS
Digital
No Data
Non-Digital

September 2009

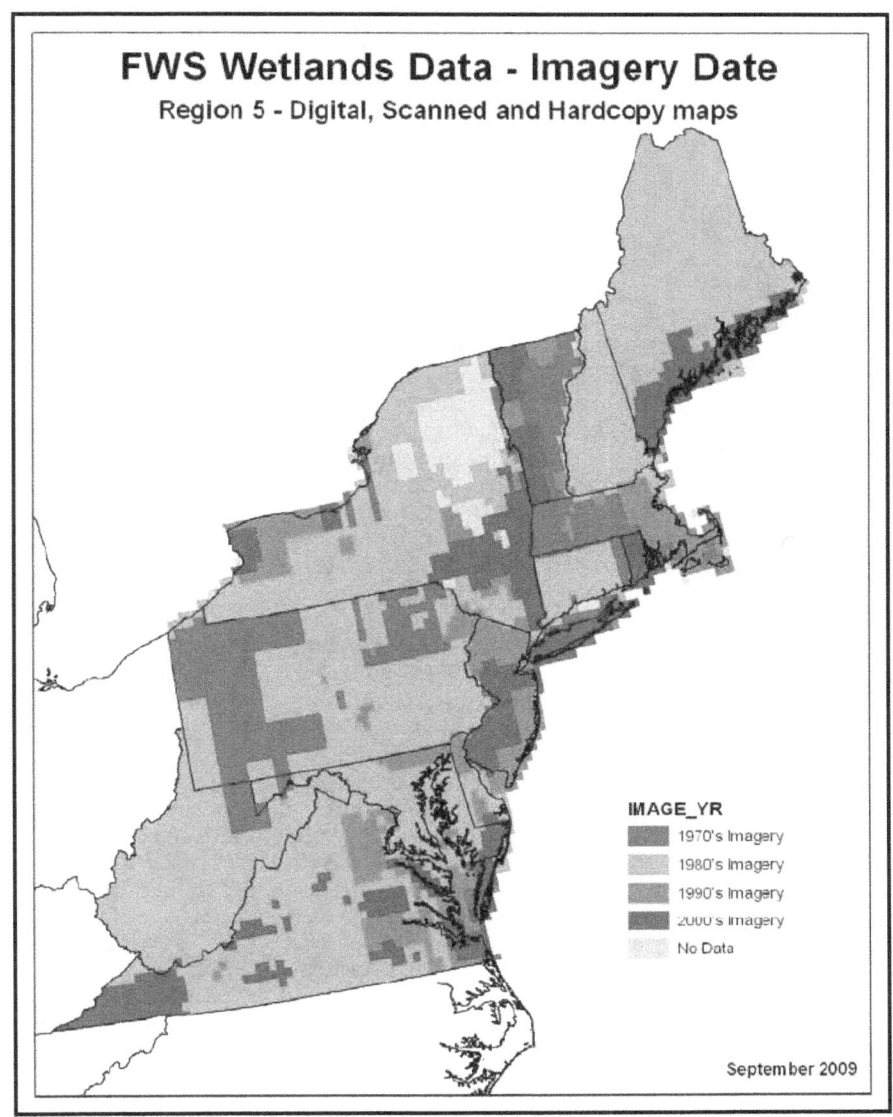

FWS Wetlands Data - Imagery Date
Region 5 - Digital, Scanned and Hardcopy maps

IMAGE_YR
1970's Imagery
1980's Imagery
1990's Imagery
2000's Imagery
No Data

September 2009

FY09 Mapping Activities. Mapping work included Long Island, New York (51 quads) and Sussex County, Delaware (27 quads). Data for the former were finalized and entered into the wetlands master geospatial database, while the Delaware work is in review.

Mapping In Progress for FY2010. As part of a national initiative to update NWI data for coastal refuges, NWI data for the following refuges will be updated: Back Bay (MD), Blackwater (MD), Cape May (NJ), Eastern Neck (MD), Monomoy (MA), Parker River (MA), Stewart B. McKinney (CT), Supawna Meadows (NJ), and Edwin B. Forsythe (NJ). The Regional

Refuge Program provided funds for updating NWI data for additional refuges: Presquile (VA), James River (VA), Great Bay (NH), Sunkhaze (ME), Pondicherry (NH), Canaan Valley (WV), Erie/French Creek (PA), Moosehorn (ME), and the Potomac River complex (VA). NWI data for New Jersey will be updated with 2007 imagery using a rapid assessment technique that is being evaluated for future use where high-quality NWI data exist. This effort will allow the R5 NWI to prepare a new state wetlands report that will provide current wetland acreage summaries, and the results of enhanced NWI data including a statewide preliminary assessment of wetland functions.

FY09 Special Projects.

Local Wetland Trends Analysis. R5 NWI conducted a wetland trends study for the Delaware and Catskills watersheds of the New York City water supply system (funded by NY City DEP).

Eelgrass Monitoring for Long Island Sound. We initiated a survey of eelgrass beds in the eastern end of Long Island Sound (funded by EPA; work will be completed in FY10). This work is part of a long-term monitoring survey that we began several years ago. Data have been updated every three years since 2003.

FY09 Presentations. 1) "Assessment of Wetland Functions Using Enhanced National Wetlands Inventory Data: Ventura River Watershed (California) and Nanticoke River Watershed (Maryland and Delaware)" (co-presenter with R1 Coordinator) at Association of State Wetland Managers Conference (October 2008): Portland, OR. 2)"Use of Remote Sensing and GIS Technology for Wetland, Riparian, and Watershed Assessment, Restoration, and Monitoring" at Southern New England Chapter of the Soil and Water Conservation Association and Soil Science Society of Southern New England Conference (February 26, 2009), Hadley, MA, 3) "National Wetlands Inventory Update for New England 2009" at Southern New England Chapter of the Soil and Water Conservation Association and Soil Science Society of Southern New England Conference (February 26, 2009), Hadley, MA, and 4) "The National Wetlands Inventory: Where We've Been and Where We Can Go" (Symposium 6: Wetland Remote Sensing and Mapping) at Society of Wetland Scientists Annual Meeting (June 23, 2009), Madison, WI.

FY09 Coordination with Others. R5 NWI has agreements with New York City Department of Environmental Protection (NYCDEP) for wetland mapping and trends analysis and with US EPA Region 2 for eelgrass survey in Long Island Sound (NY). We are working with NYCDEP on wetland booklet summarizing results of most recent NWI mapping and trends analysis and cooperating with Delaware Department of Natural Resources and Environmental Control in updating NWI data for Delaware. R5 NWI is assisting the State of California in their development of a wetland definition and classification system.

Regional Applications of NWI Data. The following are some examples of uses of NWI data.

Drinking Water Protection. The New York City Department of Environmental Protection (NYCDEP) uses NWI maps and trends data to protect wetlands important for maintaining high

water quality for New York City's 8.3 million residents and 40+ million visitors. An atlas of NWI maps was prepared and distributed to all municipalities in the City's three major watershed areas (Croton, Delaware, and Catskills) for use in local wetland protection. NYCDEP uses NWI data (including enhanced NWI data) to develop research studies evaluating water quality and the impacts of local development on this resource and in reporting to EPA on the status of wetlands. By protecting wetlands and their role in water quality renovation, NYCDEP is able to avoid the costs of filtration of reservoir waters in the Catskill/Delaware water supply, saving the City billions of dollars. The NWI data have been summarized in a public information booklet "Wetlands in the Watersheds of the New York City Water Supply System" to educate the public on wetlands, their functions, their status in the reservoir watersheds, and what can be done to help protect the remaining wetlands. NYCDEP also uses NWI data to identify wetlands that may be eligible for protection under New York State's freshwater wetland law and subject to regulation at the federal and local levels. The NWI data are also used in the design of its capital construction and for the department's forest and stream management, land acquisition, and wetland monitoring programs.

Identification of Priority Wetlands for State Regulation. For nearly two decades, the State of Vermont has used NWI maps to identify wetlands of significance that received increased protection through the Vermont Wetland Rules. In passing the Rules back in the 1990s, the State decided that any wetland shown on an NWI map would be considered a Class 2 wetland of significance. Class 1 and 2 wetlands are regulated under the Rules (Class 1 wetlands are wetlands with unique properties such as those harboring rare and endangered species, etc.). A Conditional Use Determination can only be issued if it is determined that the use will have no undue adverse impact on protected functions, unless such impacts are mitigated.

Aid to Wetland Protection Efforts. Unless replaced by more current wetland data from state or local agencies, NWI maps and data serve as the main guide for local governments across the region. Maine Department of Environmental Protection staff use the NWI maps regularly to identify and characterize sites for biological monitoring, to provide information for license and permit reviews (NRPA, Site Law, discharge permits, hydro projects), and for enforcement issues. An example of use of NWI data for local wetland protection follows. The Clinton (NY) local zoning law (local law number 2 of 2008) dealing with freshwater wetlands, watercourses, lakes, ponds, and floodplains identifies NWI maps as one of two sources of information for locating wetlands prior to conducting field investigations (the other source is the state wetland data). NWI data have been referenced in numerous local master plans as part of the natural resource component. In his book "Ecologically Based Municipal Land Use Planning" (Lewis Publishers 1999), William Honachefsky identifies NWI maps as "one of the most common maps … to be included in municipality natural resource inventory" and further recognizes enhanced NWI and its application for preliminary assessment of wetland functions as an important contribution for incorporation in local master plans. The Center for Watershed Protection (Ellicott City, MD) has also made similar recommendations regarding the use of NWI in a number of its watershed protection guidance documents designed for local governments and watershed associations.

Conservation Planning. The Service's New Jersey Field Office used NWI data and expertise to develop a conservation strategy for protecting and restoring the Hackensack Meadowlands – the largest estuarine wetland complex in northern New Jersey. The NWI contribution to the strategy included identification of wetlands and potential wetland restoration sites, a landscape-level analysis of wetland functions, and information on historic and recent wetland trends. The NWI Program prepared a report "The Hackensack River Watershed, New Jersey and New York: Wetland Characterization, Preliminary Assessment of Wetland Functions, and Remotely-sensed Indices of Natural Habitat Integrity" that served as one of the foundations for the strategy. In addition, this report is being used to develop a master plan for conserving wetlands and other natural resources within this urbanizing watershed. The Maryland Department of Natural Resources has used NWI data in preparing strategic watershed-based wetland conservation plans. When available, enhanced NWI data have been used to identify significant wetlands for performing certain functions.

Refuge Planning and Management. NWI is considered a fundamental layer used for many aspects of refuge planning and management program. Just three examples of refuge use of NWI data are cited. Canaan Valley National Wildlife Refuge (NWR) uses NWI data on a regular basis: 1) to evaluate habitat management projects and identify areas where public access can and can't be permitted, 2) to produce informal reports to realty staff working on acquisitions to show relative wetland/upland acres to support acquisition packages, and 3) to distribute survey and inventory points for sampling wetland wildlife and/or specific plant communities. The Rappahannock NWR uses NWI data: 1) to help develop goals, objectives and strategies for wetland habitat conservation in their Comprehensive Conservation Plan for the refuge, 2) to justify land acquisition funding requests to the Migratory Bird Conservation Commission, 3) to document wetlands that would be conserved in a North American Wetlands Conservation Act grant request, 4) to document wetlands that would be conserved in several applications to the Virginia Aquatic Resources Trust Fund, 5) to help determine migratory bird habitat values on lands being considered for acquisition, and 6) to help determine land use restrictions and locations of vegetated buffers to

be installed through conservation easements. Chincoteague NWR, a coastal refuge along the Atlantic Ocean, is one of many coastal NWRs that are using NWI data to run sea-level rise models that predict the effect of rising sea levels on refuge lands. As a result of this application, the refuge manager realized that the refuge boundaries need to be modified to include lands (currently lowland forests) that will likely become salt marshes as these marshes migrate landward. This information will help shape the refuge's short-term and long-term acquisition plan.

Endangered or Rare Species Habitat Conservation. The New York Natural Heritage Program (NYNHP) is using NWI data and state wetland data to target the full range of habitats potentially used by wetland-dependent species of concern. Known occurrences of these species (i.e., occupied wetlands determined by ground surveys and radio-telemetry) are combined with wetlands and uplands (as appropriate) within the known range of the species using conservative estimates to determine areas that should be conserved. These "important area" models have been developed for numerous animals including freshwater mussels, dragonflies, damselflies, Tomah mayfly *(Siphlonisca aerodromia)*, bogbean buckmoth *(Hemileuca sp.)*, devil crawfish *(Cambarus diogenes)*, bog turtle *(Clemmys muhlenbergii)*, Blanding's turtle *(Emydoidea blandingii)*, spiny softshell turtle *(Trionyx spiniferus)*, queen snake *(Regina septemvittata)*, eastern massasauga *(Sistrurus catenatus catenatus)*, northern cricket frog *(Acris crepitans)*, longtail salamander *(Eurycea longicauda)*, marsh birds (including pied-billed grebe *Podilymbus podiceps*, least bittern Ixobrychus exilis, and rails), common tern *(Sterna hirundo)*, and several fishes.

Twenty-six endangered mussels and fish inhabit the Upper Tennessee River Basin in the Clinch, Powell, and Holston River Drainages. Home of one of the most diverse freshwater mussel and fish communities in the Nation, this area contains over

85 species of mussels and 149 fish species native to this Basin and some are found nowhere else. To contribute to their recovery, the NWI mapped wetlands, waters, and riparian corridors in these watersheds. The Service has been working vigorously with state resource agencies, soil and water conservation districts, local watershed groups, other non-government organizations, and other federal agencies to restore and protect these trust resources through cooperative partnerships. These data are being used to identify high priority areas, plan for restoration of riparian habitats to improve water quality and reduce sedimentation, identify and define threats, provide baseline data for future trend analysis, and provide a prospective for watershed-based protection and restoration.

Research. NWI data have been used by numerous researchers to identify wetlands for studying wetland wildlife and for environmental analysis. One such study investigated salt marsh bird diversity in New England and Long Island, New York (Shriver et al. 2004). NWI data were used to identify potential estuarine emergent wetland sites for this regional study of bird breeding in salt marshes. The State of Maine's biomonitoring program uses NWI data for GIS spatial analysis for a variety of projects including water quality predictive model development and support of total maximum daily loads (TMDLs) analysis. Researchers at the U.S. Geological Survey are using NWI data to quantify wetlands on the landscape that may be influencing the flux of organic carbon from rivers to the Gulf of Maine.

Regional Wetland Publications. The following is a list of some of the more significant wetland publications produced by the Region's NWI program, mainly state and regional wetland reports. The Region has produced numerous other publications on the results of the NWI (e.g., local status reports, local trend analyses, and watershed-based wetland characterizations and preliminary functional assessments of wetlands); contact the Regional Coordinator for a copy of the regional wetland publications list.

Tiner, R.W. 2007. Maine Wetlands and Waters: Results of the National Wetlands Inventory. U.S. Fish and Wildlife Service, Northeast Region, Hadley, MA. NWI Technical Report. 22 pp.

Tiner, R.W. 2007. New Hampshire Wetlands and Waters: Results of the National Wetlands Inventory. U.S. Fish and Wildlife Service, Northeast Region, Hadley, MA. NWI Technical Report. 21 pp.

Tiner, R.W. 1996. West Virginia's Wetlands: Uncommon, Valuable Wildlands. U.S. Fish and Wildlife Service, Ecological Services, Northeast Region, Hadley, MA. 20 pp.

Tiner, R.W., and D.G. Burke. 1995. Wetlands of Maryland. U.S. Fish and Wildlife Service, Ecological Services, Region 5, Hadley, MA and Maryland Department of Natural Resources, Annapolis, MD. Cooperative publication. 193 pp. plus appendices.

Metzler, K., and R.W. Tiner. 1991. Wetlands of Connecticut. State Geological and Natural History Survey of Connecticut, Dept. of Environmental Protection, Hartford, CT in Cooperation with U.S. Fish and Wildlife Service, National Wetlands Inventory. Report of Investigations No. 13. 115 pp.

Tiner, R.W., Jr. 1989. Wetlands of Rhode Island. U.S. Fish and Wildlife Service, National Wetlands Inventory Project, Newton Corner, MA. 71 pp. plus Appendix.

Tiner, R.W., Jr., and J.T. Finn. 1986. Status and Recent Trends of Wetlands in Five Mid-Atlantic States: Delaware, Maryland, Pennsylvania, Virginia, and West Virginia. U.S. Fish and Wildlife Service, Region 5, National Wetlands Inventory Project, Newton Corner, MA and U.S. Environmental Protection Agency, Region III, Philadelphia, PA. Cooperative publication. 40 pp.

Tiner, R.W., Jr. 1985. Wetlands of Delaware. U.S. Fish and Wildlife Service, Newton Corner, MA and Delaware Dept. of Natural Resources and Environmental

Control, Dover. Cooperative publication. 77 pp.

Tiner, R.W., Jr. 1985. Wetlands of New Jersey. U.S. Fish and Wildlife Service, Newton Corner, MA. 117 pp.

Region 6: Mountain-Prairie
by Kevin Bon
Regional Wetland Coordinator
USFWS, Lakewood, CO

Current Mapping Status. NWI data have been produced for about 80 percent of the Region (the largest Service Region in the U.S.). Data are available in both map and digital formats. Fifty-seven percent of the Region has NWI data in digital format for computer applications. The remaining NWI data are mylar/paper maps or delineated photography; they are being digitized and added to the wetlands master geospatial database as funding becomes available.

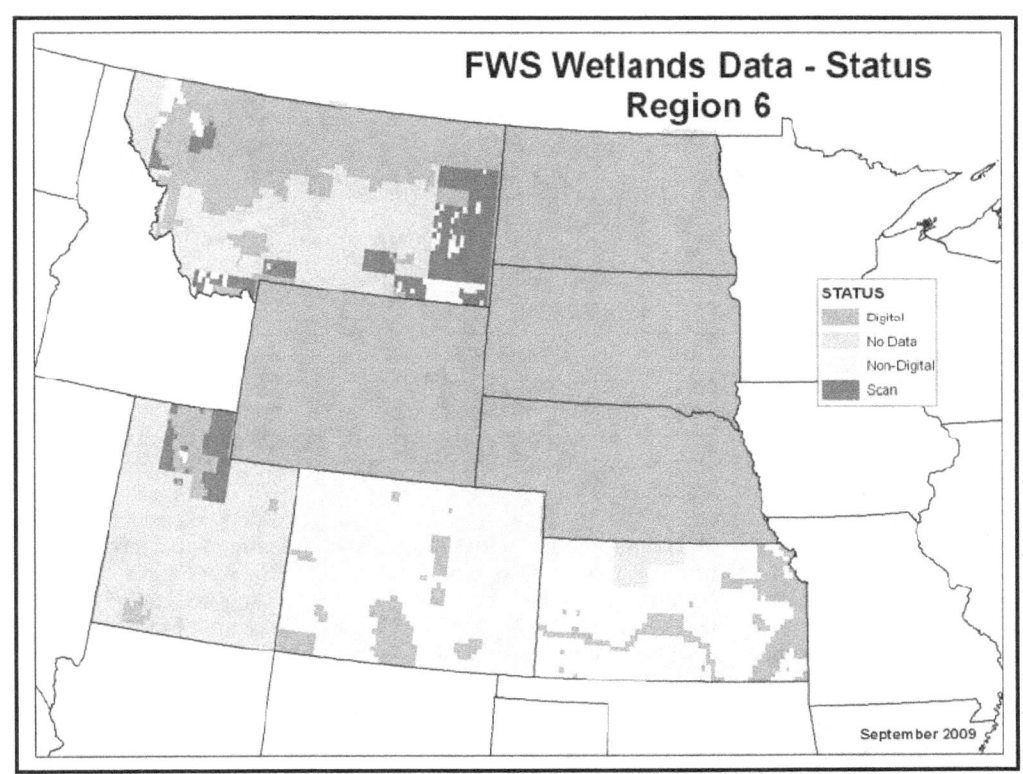

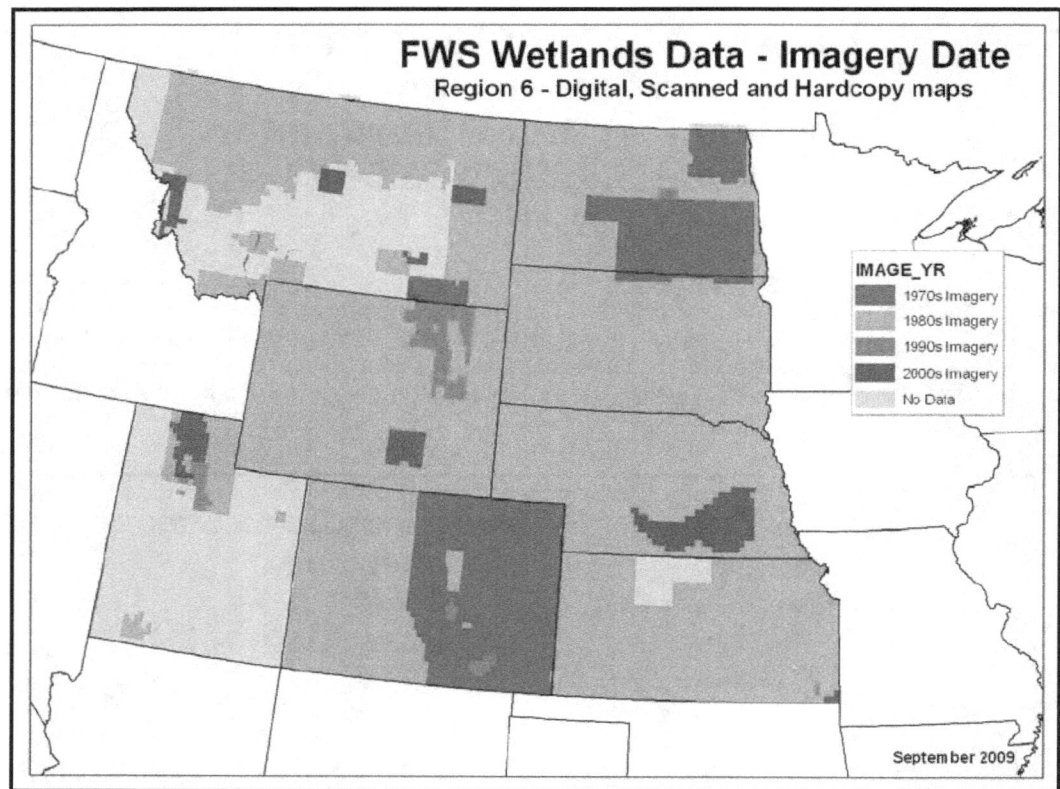

FY09 Mapping Activities. Updated NWI data were produced for Nebraska's Rainwater Basin and Wyoming's Shirley Basin and the remaining portion of the Powder River Basin. The remaining hardcopy maps in Wyoming were converted to digital data to complete digital NWI data for the state. Two small project areas in Montana were mapped: an area in central Montana and the other in the southeastern part of the state.

Mapping In Progress for FY2010. Additional areas in Montana will be mapped by the Montana Natural Heritage Program. NWI data for Wells County, North Dakota will be updated for use by the Region's Habitat and Population Evaluation Team. Digitizing NWI data is planned for the northeastern corner of Utah and for three areas in Colorado (North Platte River, Rio Grande Headwaters, and Gilpin County). The former area will nearly complete a digital database for the Upper Colorado Shrub Steppe Strategic Habitat Conservation focal area.

Updating of Wells County, North

Dakota will be completed for the Habitat and Population Evaluation Team to show the current status of wetlands, and possible restorable wetlands.

FY09 Coordination with Others. We are working with the Montana Department of Environmental Quality, Montana Natural Heritage Program, and multiple other partners to map major portions of the state. This work includes new mapping and updating of existing NWI data. Approximately one-quarter of the state (the third largest in the contiguous United States) is currently under contract with more areas being added every year. Completion of digitizing and updating of mapping in Wyoming was done in cooperation with the Wyoming Department of Environmental Quality and the U.S. Environmental Protection Agency. We will be working with the Colorado Natural Heritage Program to digitize NWI data for priority areas in the state.

Regional Applications of NWI Data. The following are some examples of uses of NWI data.

Wildlife Habitat Conservation. NWI maps were used in North Dakota to locate nesting sites for the endangered Piping Plover. The Unconsolidated Shore class (US) along lakes corresponds to the exact habitat preferred by this bird. EPA and local and state partners are using updated NWI data along the Wasatch Front and Great Salt Lake to identify waterfowl and shorebird feeding preferences in order to develop alternate wetland futures in the rapidly expanding urban corridor around Salt Lake City. Recently updated NWI data for the Rainwater Basin are being used for landscape-level wildlife conservation planning as part of the Service's Strategic Habitat Conservation initiative for this important waterfowl production area. NWI data provide the Division of Refuges and its cooperators with current wetland data to estimate existing and potential migratory waterfowl habitat in this priority landscape.

State Wetland Conservation. The State of Montana and partners are using updated and new NWI data for a number of purposes including: identifying wetlands and intermittent streams not protected by the recently limited Clean Water Act, identifying change and ecological functions of wetlands in the Bitterroot Valley, and identifying wetland and riparian habitat change along the Yellowstone River. These applications better inform agencies and the public on the current status and threats to wetlands and riparian habitat and will aid in improving measures to insure their conservation.

Regional Wetland Publications. The following is a list of some of the more significant wetland publications produced with support from the Region's NWI program.

Elliott, C.R. and M.M. Hektner. 2000. Wetland Resources of Yellowstone National Park. Yellowstone National Park, Wyoming. 32 pp.

Johnson, R.R., K.F. Higgins, M.L. Kjellsen, and C.R. Elliott. 1997 Eastern South Dakota Wetlands. South Dakota State University, Brookings, SD. 28 pp.

Johnson, R.R. and K.F. Higgins. 1997. Wetland Resources of Eastern South Dakota. South Dakota State University, Brookings, SD. 102 pp.

Region 7: Alaska
by Jerry Tande
Regional Wetland Coordinator
USFWS, Region 7, Anchorage, AK

Current Mapping Status. Forty percent of Region 7 (R7) has been mapped covering 147.320 million acres with 30 percent available digitally via the internet. The remaining mylar/paper finals of previously mapped areas are being digitized as time permits and added to the wetlands master geospatial database as funding becomes available. Nearly all of R7 mapping has been accomplished utilizing 1978-1986, 1:60,000-scale, color-infrared imagery collected as part of the Alaska High Altitude Photography Acquisition Program (AHAP). Selective updates using more recent and finer-scale imagery have been completed for most major population centers (e.g., Anchorage-Mat-Su Boroughs, Kenai, Juneau, and Fairbanks) and a few remote areas subject to natural resource exploration and extraction (e.g., National Petroleum Reserve and Arctic Coastal Plain). The older AHAP imagery has been adequate for wetlands baseline inventory mostly due to the largely undisturbed nature of the Region. However, the need for more current imagery may become more important for addressing changes and impacts of further resource development and the effects of a changing climate.

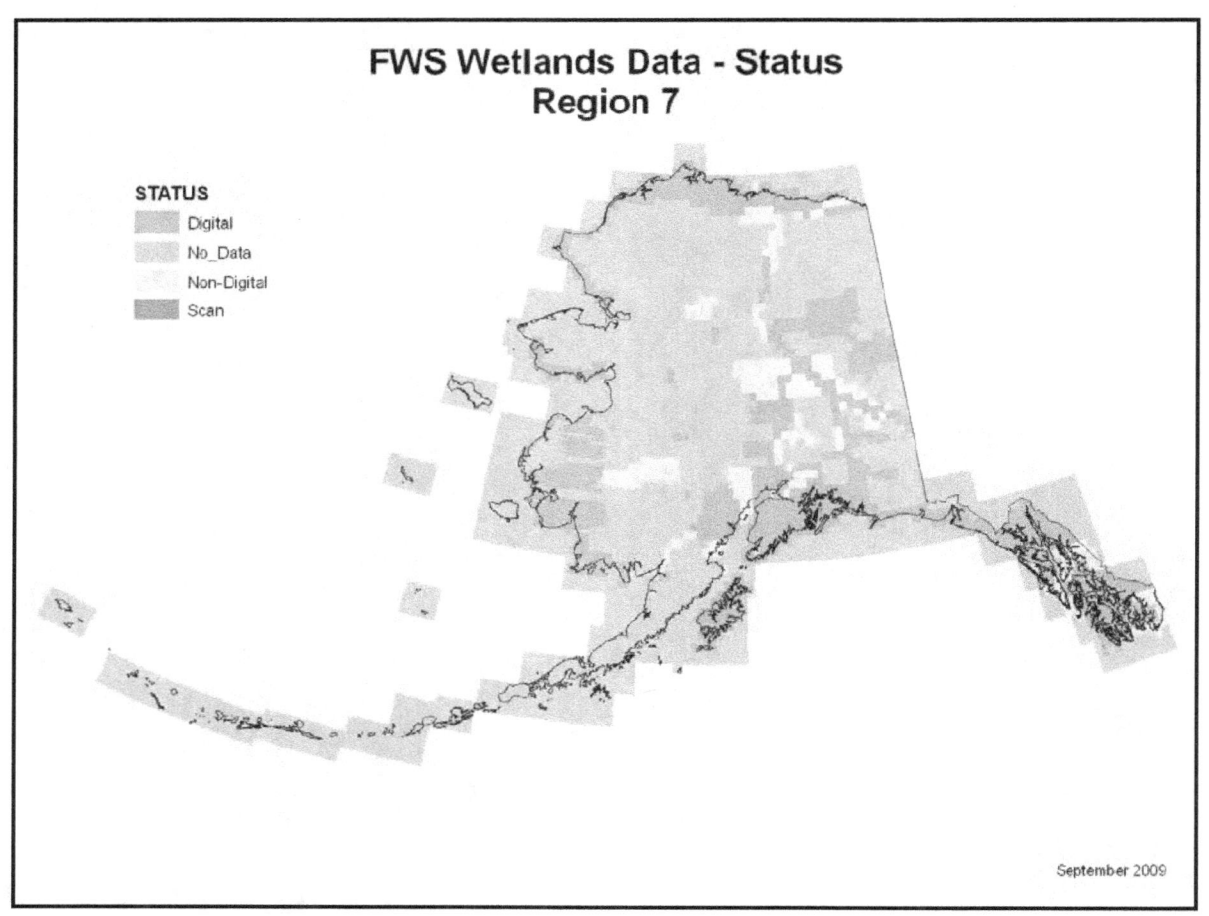

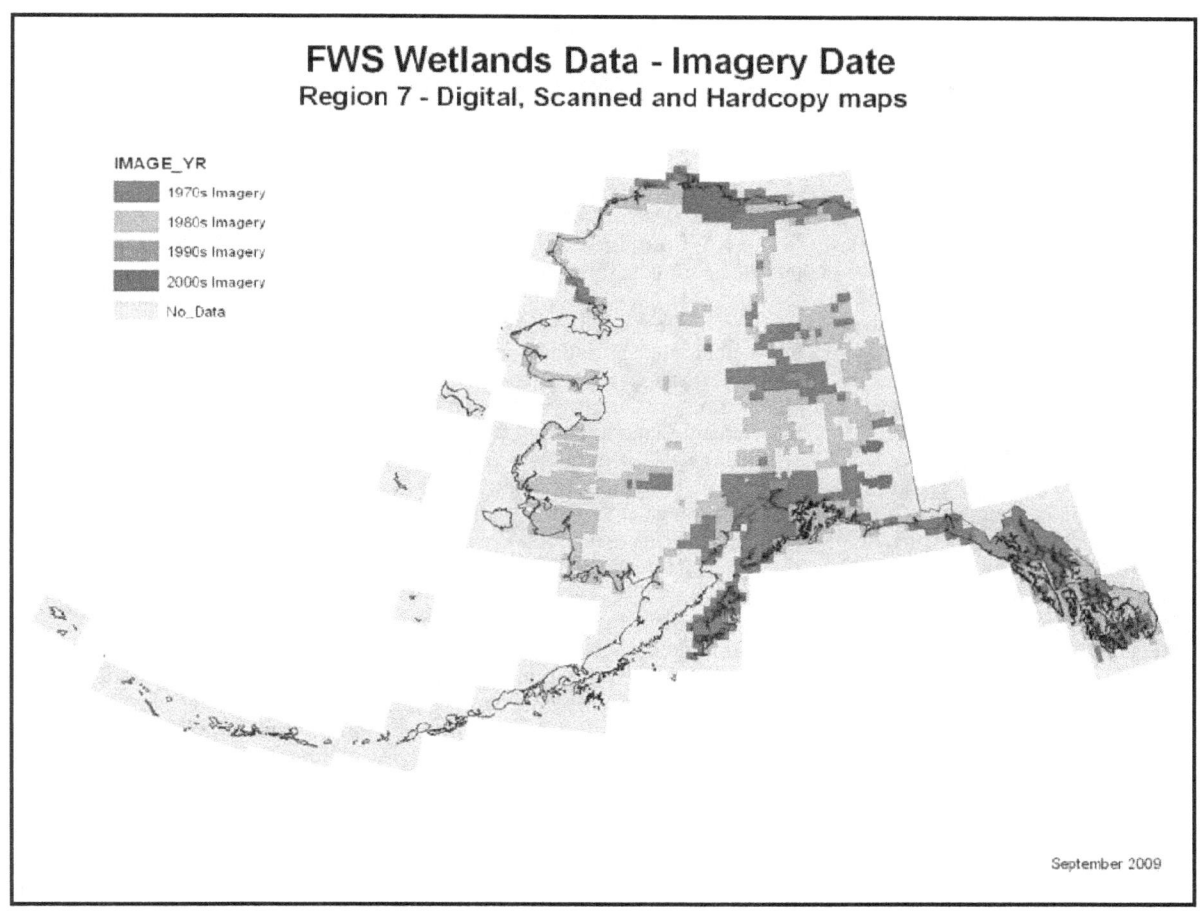

FWS Wetlands Data - Imagery Date
Region 7 - Digital, Scanned and Hardcopy maps

IMAGE_YR
- 1970s Imagery
- 1980s Imagery
- 1990s Imagery
- 2000s Imagery
- No_Data

September 2009

FY09 Mapping Activities. Due to lack of funding, no new mapping was initiated or completed in R7 in FY09. Climate change funding, however, allowed for digitizing all previously mapped northwest Arctic coastal quadrangles (covering 4.597 million acres) and adding these data to the Wetlands Mapper. These quads extended from south of Barrow along the northwest Alaska coastline to east of Nome on the Seward Peninsula, and are intended to support coastal change analysis, wetland gains/losses and migratory bird habitat changes related to climate change. The coastal Chukchi Sea quads are anticipated to be used by the Service and its partners for energy-related project reviews along the coastline of Alaska's newest and largest offshore oil and gas lease sale.

FY09 Special Projects.

Arctic Coastal Change Analysis for the Yukon-Kuskokwim Delta Refuge: An assessment of changing coastal shorelines and estuarine and lacustrine wetland habitat types along the Bering Sea coast, Yukon Delta National Wildlife Refuge (YKD) is being conducted utilizing 2007-08 Ikonos, 1988 color, 1978-86 CIR, and 1950s B&W imagery. The study area encompasses the most productive portion of the western Arctic coast within the YKD, supporting one of the largest aggregations of shorebirds and waterbirds in the world, including significant fractions of the Pacific and world populations of Pacific black brant, cackling Canada geese, and emperor geese, as well as critical habitat for threatened spectacled and Steller's eiders. Because of its expansive, low-elevation coastal areas, much of the Refuge and its critical habitats are at risk of sea-level rise and other affects of accelerated warming.

Creation of a Database to Monitor Changes of Cook Inlet Coastal Marsh Habitats: NWI initiated work to create a database for monitoring changes of coastal marsh habitats in Cook Inlet (south central Alaska). Work began with the establishment of a GIS database of currently available vegetation data for Westchester Lagoon in Anchorage. Construction of a fish passageway on Westchester was completed as part of a program for the reintroduction of a salmon run to Chester Creek. NWI, in partnership with the Anchorage Field Office and Coastal Program FWS, collected vegetation data and completed photo interpretation for coastal Westchester Lagoon. These data will form the basis for retrospective change analysis, modeling of habitat change trajectories, and a baseline for future comparative work of the fish passageway construction area. It is also anticipated to provide educational materials and GIS opportunities for local schools.

To lay the groundwork for cooperative efforts and to ensure that new mapping captures biologically significant changes,

NWI initiated work to align current vegetation data with NWI mapping conventions and an existing Ecological Land Survey for south central Alaska. It is anticipated that this scalable mapping effort, centered in Anchorage, would be expandable to include all coastal marshes in the Anchorage Borough. As funding becomes available, it is envisioned that future work might be expanded to include upper and lower Cook Inlet and incorporate this comprehensive classification system contained within the GIS database.

Fairbanks Status and Trends Assessment: A Fairbanks status and trends project is being conducted by a graduate student with the assistance of the R7 Fairbanks Field Office and NWI staff. A field guide to the photo interpretation and mapping conventions and associated plant communities was completed and reviewed for its application by R7 staff, the Corp of Engineers and a Fairbanks wetlands consultant in 2008/2009. Status mapping is scheduled for completion October 2009, with trends studies scheduled for completion July 2010.

The Fairbanks area is experiencing considerable growth, particularly in areas that are predominantly wetland. In order to educate local decision-makers to the value of conserving remaining wetlands, wetland losses must first be quantified and the ecological implications of these losses described. The database will be employed to collaborate with the Corps, the Borough and other agencies to identify key wetlands in need of conservation. As a major planning tool, the GIS database will become the baseline for assessing the acreage, locations and types of wetlands lost in the Fairbanks area since 1949. In addition to quantifying wetlands changes, an assessment of the function and fish and wildlife value of specifically impacted wetlands will accompany the final report.

Strategic Habitat Conservation Planning – Matanuska-Susitna Borough: NWI staff are actively involved with ongoing, more detailed wetland map updates - including

aspects of wetland functional assessments - with a Borough-Corp of Engineers contractor. R7-NWI completed a NWI national pilot project in 2009 in the Mat-Su Borough to test the enhancement of NWI data in Alaska. The method added new descriptors (LLWW) to the NWI database: landscape position (L); landform (L); water flow path (W); and waterbody type (W). These values may allow performing landscape-level functional assessments, help assess significance of wetland losses, and predict functions expected from potential wetland restoration efforts. A report and a geodatabase were prepared for the project. The report provides observations on the application of LLWW in south central Alaska.

An ongoing cooperative effort between the Borough and NWI is anticipated to provide improved registration of NWI data utilizing more recent photography and the services of the Mat-Su Planning Department's GIS team. Fully funded by the Borough, this contributor's data covering 2.2 million acres would meet current national mapping standards and be completed spring 2010.

Digitizing Historic Alaska Status and Trends Plots: Studies were conducted between 1985 and 1994 to develop statewide statistical estimates of the aeral extent of wetlands and deepwater habitats for Alaska utilizing 2,566 four-square mile plots. The original plot delineations and wetland polygon boundaries are on hard-copy mylar overlays on unrectified aerial photography. These sample units were never digitized; however, future work on the status and trends (S&T) of Alaska's wetlands and linkages to ongoing status and trends of the Nation's wetlands will depend upon the use of these sample units once they have been scanned, vectorized, attributed and incorporated into a GIS database. The dataset has additional applications to EPA and their EMAP wetland condition monitoring program in Alaska since NWI S&T plots form the basis for their plot locations. A pilot EPA project is proposed for 2010 on the

North Slope. The NWI plots also might potentially be considered for broad assessments of climate change effects in the Region.

The goal of the FY09 project was to provide an assessment of the costs and issues faced in bringing a sample of these historic plots into the digital age. A subset of approximately 200 sample units were scanned, vectorized, attributed and incorporated into a GIS layer. Sample units were prioritized for the northern and western Arctic coastal areas with further priority given to plots falling within areas of more recent imagery acquisitions (e.g., 2007-2008 Ikonos, Yukon Delta Refuge; BLM 2003 CIR, central Arctic coastal plain). A report accompanies a geodatabase for the project.

FY09 Coordination with Others. R7 NWI staff participate in a number of committees or groups dealing with the effect of climate change including regional office subcommittees dealing with species and habitat change forecasting, and sea-level rise and physical hazards assessment; a cooperators group for western Arctic coastal change analysis and for assessing wetland habitat gains, losses and changes; a regional group addressing the technical needs and talents necessary for Regional Landscape Conservation Regions (LCRs); regional GIS committee. We are also working with: 1) an interagency cooperative group identifying agency needs and exploring solutions for imagery acquisition for statewide 1:24K ortho-image base maps and digital elevation models that meet NWI's National Mapping Standards, 2) USGS-Alaska Science Center on a large coastal change model proposal for Cook Inlet west of Anchorage that may involve a wetlands layer update, 3) refuge management of the Alaska Peninsula/Becharof Refuges to develop a plan to complete wetlands mapping of the Bristol Bay/Alaska Peninsula region, 4) Matanuska Susitna Borough, Corps of Engineers and EPA on wetlands-related issues, and Borough GIS staff in their efforts to adjust existing NWI data to new ortho-photo base registration (see FY09

Special Projects above), 5) Alaska DEC and R10-EPA implementing an EPA wetlands condition assessment (EMAP) pilot project for FY10 providing R7-NWI status and trends plot information, and 6) the state DOT committee in rewriting their wetlands assessment and hydrogeomorphic manual.

Regional Applications of NWI Data. The following are some examples of uses of NWI data.

Sea-level Rise Impact Assessment. National Wildlife Federation, partnering with the US Fish and Wildlife Service's Coastal Program, is incorporating NWI data to a SLAMM analysis to map sea level rise impacts on Cook Inlet coastal habitats, create a report on the results, and use that report as the basis for a conference discussing the findings and applications of SLAMM in Alaska, and implications for fish and wildlife managers. It also will provide a good opportunity to develop information useful to a wide-range of Cook Inlet resource issues while educating the public about global warming impacts and helping agencies and NGOs grapple with difficulties of incorporating climate change into management decisions. Cook Inlet is part of R7's south-central Alaska Focal Area for Strategic Habitat Conservation and Green Infrastructure activities. South-central is also home to nearly 3/4s of the State's population.

Conservation Planning. The Nature Conservancy used the NWI database of estuarine and marine coastal data in their "Conservation Assessment and Resource Synthesis for Southeast Alaska and the Tongass National Forest" recently published at http://conserveonline.org/workspaces/akcfm as a systematic assessment of biodiversity values, habitat conditions and conservation status for the bioregion, and for providing recommendations for how these findings can be applied to improve conservation within the Tongass National Forest.

Contaminant Effect on Wildlife Investigations. NWI maps and digital data have been used by

the FWS Anchorage Field Office to identify wood frog habitat for contaminants-related studies.

Wildlife Studies. NWI digital data have been used by USGS Alaska Sciences Center to identify critical Vancouver Canada geese estuarine use areas in southeast Alaska. Besides the identification of critical habitat areas, use of NWI data allowed for narrowing the flyover areas necessary for completing accurate inventory and monitoring counts by expensive aircraft. NWI data have been used by USGS Alaska Sciences Center for habitat identification and assessment of sea ducks in southeast Alaska.

Environmental Impact Statements. Digital NWI data were used by Wrangell St. Elias National Park in EIS preparations for an all-terrain vehicle land cover damage assessment within the Park (wetland identification, condition assessments, buffer determinations, and reclamation efforts).

Regional Wetland Publications. The following is a list of some of the more significant wetland publications produced by the Region's NWI program. Other publications may be available; contact the Regional Coordinator for a complete listing.

Hall, J.V. 2001. Status and trends of wetlands in the Palmer/Wasilla area, Alaska (1978 to 1996). Prepared for U.S. Environmental Protection Agency, Region 10, Alaska Operations Office, 222 W. Seventh Avenue #19, Anchorage, AK. U.S. Fish and Wildlife Service, National Wetlands Inventory, Region 7, Anchorage, AK. 21 pp.

Hall, J.V. 1988. Alaska Coastal Wetlands Survey. Cooperative Report: Dept. of the Interior, U.S. Fish and Wildlife Service, National Wetlands Inventory, Washington, DC. and Dept. of Commerce, National Oceanic and Atmospheric Administration, National Ocean Service, National Marine Pollution Program Office, 11400 Rockville Pike, Rockville, MD. U.S. Fish and Wildlife Service, National Wetlands Inventory, Region 7, Anchorage, AK. 36 pp.

Hall, J.V. and S.E. Kratzer. 2001. Status and Trends of Wetlands in the Lower Kenai River Area, Alaska (1950 to 1996). Prepared for U.S. Environmental Protection Agency, Region 10, Alaska Operations Office, 222 W. Seventh Avenue No. 19, Anchorage, AK. U.S. Fish and Wildlife Service, National Wetlands Inventory, Region 7, Anchorage, AK. 16 pp.

Hall, J.V., W.E. Frayer and W.O. Wilen. 1994. Status of Alaska Wetlands. U.S. Fish and Wildlife Service, National Wetlands Inventory, Region 7, Anchorage, AK. 33 pp.

Hall, J.V., B. Keating, S. Kratzer, T.W. Jennings and L. Nakazawa. 1996. Alaska Wetlands and Hydrography. Prepared for Government Applications Task Force, Central Intelligence Committee and Civil Applications Committee. U.S. Fish and Wildlife Service, National Wetlands Inventory, Region 7, Anchorage, AK. 39 pp.

Washington Office Activities: FY2009
by Bill Wilen
USFWS, Region 9, Washington, DC

The Washington Office (WO-NWI) pursues applications of NWI data by the Service and other Federal agencies, especially in matters concerning environmental policies. Some of their activities are outlined below.

Making the Service's Wetlands Classification System and Mapping Conventions Federal Standards. The Department of the Interior through the Fish and Wildlife Service has been assigned responsible for developing the digital wetlands layer of the Spatial Data Infrastructure by OMB Circular A-16. This action is being done through the Federal Geographic Data Committee's Wetland Subcommittee chaired by WO-NWI staff. The Service's wetland definition has been the federal standard for identifying the limit of biological wetlands since 1996. On July 7, 2009 the Wetlands Mapping Standard was adopted as the national standard. It was developed by the Wetlands Subcommittee built on the mapping conventions used by the NWI. The new standard is designed to guide current and future wetlands mapping projects and enhance the overall quality and consistency of wetlands data. Quality data on wetlands are considered critical for planning effective conservation strategies to benefit fish and wildlife resources now and in the future.

Coordination with the Department of Housing and Urban Development (HUD). HUD's Office of Environment sent their President Management Fellow (PMF) over to the Service for a rotational assignment with WO-NWI staff. The intent was for their PMF to gain enough wetland knowledge to write a HUD guidebook on wetlands or to recommend wetland regulations for the agency. At their national meeting, the Office of Environment

proposed to use the Service's wetland definition in their draft wetlands rule. They recognize that the Service's wetland classification system identifies the biological limit of wetlands and is broader than the jurisdictional limit and is therefore more useful for their programs.

Supporting the Use and Development of Sea Level Affecting Marshes Model (SLAMM). Since SLAMM uses NWI data to identify wetlands that may be impacted by sea-level rise, NWI staff has been involved since the model's development in 1985. Currently, SLAMM has evolved to version 5. WO-NWI staff were instrumental in getting SLAMM data posted online and have been working with the Service's Refuge Program in applying SLAMM to coastal refuges. The refuges will use these data to assist in planning for the likely adverse impacts of sea-level rise on coastal wetlands, neighboring nontidal wetlands, and low-lying uplands. WO-NWI proposed and received funding for a three-year $300,000 science support project funded the U.S. Geological Survey to help develop the scientific foundations for future versions of SLAMM.

WO-NWI has been deeply involved with development of an on-line viewer called "SLAMM-View" from inception. For most SLAMM simulations, an output file is produced for each of five different dates in a time-series (i.e., Base Year, 2025, 2050, 2075, and 2100) for three different scenario of sea-level rise (e.g., IPCC A1B Mean, IPCC A1B Max, and 1m). When examining these outputs, interested parties logically most often want to view two types of combinations of these 15 different data layers: "same scenario, different date", and "same date, different scenario", which

in sum result in 45 unique pairs of simulation output. This is not feasible without a viewer. SLAMM-View is a browser-based application that accesses contextual layers such as state and county boundaries, roads, and NWI wetlands via web mapping services, with adjustable layer transparency and a layer-control view that allows users to order and turn these ancillary layers on and off. One unique aspect of this web-mapping tool, vital to facilitating a comparison between the selected pair of simulation results, is that the dual maps are geographically-linked: zooming or panning in one map causes an identical action in the other map. SLAMM-view was the featured tool at NOAA's spring 2009 Geo Tools Conference.

Assists in National Policy Interpretation. WO-NWI staff represented the Service on the writing team for the proposed new Floodplain Executive Order and serves as a member of the Interagency Ocean Policy Task Force's Data Integration and Management Subgroup.

References

Ciminelli, J. and J. Scrivani. 2007. Virginia Conservation Lands Needs Assessment: Virginia Watershed Integrity Model. Virginia Department of Conservation and Recreation-Division of Natural Heritage, Virginia Department of Forestry, Virginia Commonwealth University-Center for Environmental Studies, and Virginia Department of Environmental Quality-Coastal Zone Management Program. http://www.dcr.virginia.gov/natural_heritage/vclnawater.shtml

Cowardin, L.M., V. Carter, F.C. Golet, and E.T. LaRoe. 1979. Classification of Wetlands and Deepwater Habitats of the United States. U.S. Fish and Wildlife Service, Washington, DC. FWS-OBS/79-61. 131 pp. http://library.fws.gov/FWS-OBS/79_31.pdf

Dahl, T.E. 2006. Status and Trends of Wetlands in the Conterminous United States 1998 to 2004. U.S. Department of the Interior, Fish and Wildlife Service, Washington, DC. 112 pp. http://library.fws.gov/Pubs9/wetlands98-04.pdf

Dahl, T.E. 2000. Status and Trends of Wetlands in the Conterminous United States 1986 to 1997. U.S. Department of the Interior, Fish and Wildlife Service, Washington, DC. 82 pp. http://library.fws.gov/Pubs9/wetlands86-97_lowres.pdf

Dahl, T.E. and C.E. Johnson. 1991. Status and Trends of Wetlands in the Conterminous United States mid-1970s to mid-1980s. U.S. Department of the Interior, Fish and Wildlife Service, Washington, DC. 28 pp. http://library.fws.gov/Pubs9/Wetlands70s80s.pdf

Dahl, T.E., J. Dick, J. Swords, and B.O. Wilen. 2009. Data Collection Requirements and Procedures for Mapping Wetland, Riparian and Related Habitats of the United States. U.S. Fish and Wildlife Service, Office of Habitat and Resource Conservation, National Standards and Support Team, Madison, WI. http://www.fws.gov/wetlands/_documents/gNSDI/DataCollectionRequirementsProcedures.pdf

FGDC Wetlands Subcommittee. 2009. Wetland Mapping Standard. Federal Geographic Data Committee Document Number FGDC-STD-015-2009. http://www.fws.gov/wetlands/_documents/gNSDI/FGDCWetlandsMappingStandard.pdf

Frayer, W.E., T.J. Monahan, D.C. Bowden, and F.A. Graybill. 1983. Status and Trends of Wetlands and Deepwater Habitats in the Conterminous United States 1950's to 1970's. Department of Forest and Wood Sciences, Colorado State University, Ft. Collins, CO.

McKenzie, P.M. 2005[2006]. Using the National Wetland Inventory as a tool to locate fens and other rare Missouri wetland natural communities. Missouriensis 26:36-39.

McKenzie, P.M. 2005. Using the National Wetlands Inventory as a tool for endangered species conservation. Association of State Wetland Managers, Windham, ME. www.aswm.org/wbn/archive/05/050531c.doc

Shriver, W.G., T.P. Hodgman, J.P. Gibbs, and P.D. Vickery. 2004. Landscape context influences salt marsh bird diversity and area requirements in New England. Biological Conservation 119: 545-553.

Tiner, R.W. 1984. Wetlands of the United States: Current Status and Recent Trends. U.S. Department of the Interior, Fish and Wildlife Service, Washington, DC. 59 pp. http://www.fws.gov/wetlands/_documents/gSandT/NationalReports/WetlandsUSCurrentStatusRecentTrends1984.pdf

Tiner, R.W. 2003a. Dichotomous Keys and Mapping Codes for Wetland Landscape Position, Landform, Water Flow Path, and Waterbody Type Descriptors. U.S. Fish and Wildlife Service, Northeast Region, Hadley, MA. 44 pp. http://library.fws.gov/Wetlands/dichotomouskeys0903.pdf

Tiner, R.W. 2003b. Correlating Enhanced National Wetlands Inventory Data With Wetland Functions for Watershed Assessments: A Rationale for Northeastern U.S. Wetlands. U.S. Fish and Wildlife Service, Northeast Region, Hadley, MA. 26 pp.
http://library.fws.gov/Wetlands/corelate_wetlandsNE.pdf

References

Tiner, R.W. 2004. Remotely-sensed indicators for monitoring the general condition of "natural habitat" in watersheds: an application for Delaware's Nanticoke River watershed. Ecological Indicators 4: 227-243.

Tiner, R.W. and H.C. Bergquist. 2007. The Hackensack River Watershed, New Jersey/New York Wetland Characterization, Preliminary Assessment of Wetland Functions, and Remotely-sensed Assessment of Natural Habitat Integrity. U.S. Fish and Wildlife Service, National Wetlands Inventory, Ecological Services, Region 5, Hadley, MA. 134 pp. http://library.fws.gov/Wetlands/HackensackRiverWatershed07.pdf

U.S. Fish and Wildlife Service. 2009. The Wetlands Master Geospatial Database Annual Report 2009. Division of Habitat and Resource Conservation, National Standards and Support Team, Madison, WI.

U.S. Fish and Wildlife Service. 2002. National Wetlands Inventory: A Strategy for the 21st Century. Washington, DC. http://www.fws.gov/wetlands/_documents/gNSDI/NationalWetlandsInventoryStrategy21stCentury.pdf

U.S. Fish and Wildlife Service. 1997. A System for Mapping Riparian Areas in the Western United States. National Wetlands Inventory Program, Washington, DC. http://www.fws.gov/Wetlands/_documents/gOther/SystemMappingRiparianAreasWesternUS.pdf

Vance, L.K., K. Newlon, J. Clarke, and D.M. Stagliano. 2009. Assessment of Red Rock River Subbasin and Wetlands of the Centennial Valley. Report to the Bureau of Land Management, Montana/Dakotas State Offices. Montana Natural Heritage Program, Helena, MT. 43 pp. plus appendices. http://mtnhp.org/Reports/BLM_2009.pdf

APPENDIX A: List of Selected NWI Publications

The following is a sampling of NWI publications; these and other reports can be accessed through the internet at the NWI website (http://www.fws.gov/wetlands/) by using the "documents search engine." Some are available as online wetland publications through the Service's Conservation Library (http://library.fws.gov/WetlandPublications.html). (Note: Contact Regional Wetland Coordinators for additional publications that are not posted online.) Reports are arranged by general topics and alphabetically by author within the section. Many of the listed publications come from Region 5 (Northeast) which has produced the widest array of publications from its NWI program.

Wetland Classification

Cowardin, L.M., V. Carter, F.C. Golet, and E.T. LaRoe. 1979. Classification of Wetlands and Deepwater Habitats of the United States. U.S. Fish and Wildlife Service, Washington, DC. FWS-OBS/79-61. 131 pp.

Tiner, R.W. 2003. Dichotomous Keys and Mapping Codes for Wetland Landscape Position, Landform, Water Flow Path, and Waterbody Type Descriptors. U.S. Fish and Wildlife Service, National Wetlands Inventory Program, Northeast Region, Hadley, MA. 44 pp.

State Wetland Reports

Hall, J.V., W.E. Frayer, and B.O. Wilen. 1994. Status of Alaska Wetlands. U.S. Fish and Wildlife Service, Alaska Region, Anchorage, AK. 34 pp.

Tiner, R.W. 2007. Maine Wetlands and Waters: Results of the National Wetlands Inventory. U.S. Fish and Wildlife Service, Northeast Region, Hadley, MA. NWI Technical Report. 22 pp.

Tiner, R.W. 2007. New Hampshire Wetlands and Waters: Results of the National Wetlands Inventory. U.S. Fish and Wildlife Service, Northeast Region, Hadley, MA. NWI Technical Report. 21 pp.

Tiner, R.W. 1996. West Virginia's Wetlands: Uncommon, Valuable Wildlands. U.S. Fish and Wildlife Service, Ecological Services, Northeast Region, Hadley, MA. 20 pp.

Tiner, R.W., and D.G. Burke. 1995. Wetlands of Maryland. U.S. Fish and Wildlife Service, Ecological Services, Region 5, Hadley, MA and Maryland Department of Natural Resources, Annapolis, MD. Cooperative publication. 193 pp. plus appendices.

Metzler, K., and R.W. Tiner. 1991. Wetlands of Connecticut. State Geological and Natural History Survey of Connecticut, Dept. of Environmental Protection, Hartford, CT in Cooperation with U.S. Fish and Wildlife Service, National Wetlands Inventory. Report of Investigations No. 13. 115 pp.

Tiner, R.W., Jr. 1989. Wetlands of Rhode Island. U.S. Fish and Wildlife Service, National Wetlands Inventory Project, Newton Corner, MA. 71 pp. plus appendix.

Tiner, R.W., Jr. 1985. Wetlands of Delaware. U.S. Fish and Wildlife Service, Newton Corner, MA and Delaware Dept. of Natural Resources and Environmental Control, Dover. Cooperative publication. 77 pp.

Tiner, R.W., Jr. 1985. Wetlands of New Jersey. U.S. Fish and Wildlife Service, Newton Corner, MA. 117 pp.

Local Wetland Status Reports

Dick, J. and R. McHale. 2007. Wetland and Riparian Habitats of the Playa Lakes Region: Status Report, 2006-2007. U.S. Fish and Wildlife Service, Southwest Region 2, Albuquerque, NM. 13 pp.

Elliott, C.R. and M.M. Hektner. 2000. Wetland Resources of Yellowstone National Park. Yellowstone National Park, Wyoming. 32 pp.

Tiner, R.W. 2000. Wetlands of Staten Island, New York: Valuable Vanishing Urban Wildlands. U.S. Fish and Wildlife Service, Ecological Services, Northeast Region, Hadley, MA. Prepared for U.S. Environmental Protection Agency, Region II, New York, NY. Cooperative National Wetlands Inventory publication. 19 pp.

Tiner, R.W. 2000. Wetlands of Saratoga County, New York: Vital Resources for People and Wildlife. U.S. Fish and Wildlife Service, Ecological Services, Northeast Region, Hadley, MA. Prepared for U.S. Environmental Protection Agency, Region II, New York, NY. Cooperative National Wetlands Inventory publication. 19 pp.

Tiner, R.W. 1997. Wetlands of the Watersheds of the New York City Water Supply System. Results of the National Wetlands Inventory. U.S. Fish and Wildlife Service, Ecological Services, Northeast Region, Hadley, MA. Prepared for the N.Y. City Department of Environmental Protection, Bureau of Water Supply, Quality and Protection, Valhalla, NY. 19 pp.

Tiner, R.W., G.S. Smith, and M. Starr. 2000. Wetlands Inventory for the George Washington Memorial Parkway. U.S. Fish and Wildlife Service, Ecological Services, Northeast Region, Hadley, MA. National Wetlands Inventory Report. Prepared for the National Park Service. 26 pp.

Tiner, R.W., I.K. Huber, G.S. Smith, and M.J. Starr. 2000. Wetlands Inventory of Saratoga National Historical Park. U.S. Fish and Wildlife Service, Ecological Services, Northeast Region, Hadley, MA. National Wetlands Inventory report produced for the National Park Service. 14 pp.

National Wetland Status and Trends Reports

Dahl, T.E. 2006. Status and Trends of Wetlands in the Conterminous United States 1998 to 2004. U.S. Department of the Interior, Fish and Wildlife Service, Washington, DC. 112 pp.

Dahl, T.E. 2000. Status and Trends of Wetlands in the Conterminous United States 1986 to 1997. U.S. Department of the Interior, Fish and Wildlife Service, Washington, DC. 82 pp.

Dahl, T.E. and C.E. Johnson. 1991. Status and Trends of Wetlands in the Conterminous United States mid-1970s to mid-1980s. U.S. Department of the Interior, Fish and Wildlife Service, Washington, DC. 28 pp.

Frayer, W.E., T.J. Monahan, D.C. Bowden, and F.A. Graybill. 1983. Status and Trends of Wetlands and Deepwater Habitats in the Conterminous United States 1950's to 1970's. Department of Forest and Wood Sciences, Colorado State University, Ft. Collins, CO. 32 pp.

Tiner, R.W. 1984. Wetlands of the United States: Current Status and Recent Trends. U.S. Department of the Interior, Fish and Wildlife Service, Washington, DC. 59 pp.

Regional, State and Local Wetland Trends Reports

Dahl, T.E. 2005. Florida's Wetlands: An Update on Status and Trends 1985 to 1996. U.S. Department of the Interior, Fish and Wildlife Service, Washington, DC. 80 pp.

Dahl, T.E. 1999. South Carolina's Wetlands: Status and Trends, 1982-1989. U.S. Department of the Interior, Fish and Wildlife Service, Washington, DC. 58 pp.

Dick, J. and R. McHale. 2006. Monitoring Changes to Wetlands and Riparian Vegetation Resulting from the February 13, 2005 Flood Event, Upper Gila River, Arizona. U.S. Fish and Wildlife Service, Southwest Region 2, Albuquerque, NM. 21 pp.

Frayer, W.E., D.D. Peters, and H.R. Pywell. 1989. Wetlands of the California Central Valley, Status and Trends – 1939 to mid-1980s. U.S. Fish and Wildlife Service, Region 1, Portland, OR. 27 pp.

Frayer, W.E. and J.M. Hefner. 1991. Florida Wetlands Status and Trends, 1970s to 1980s. U.S. Fish and Wildlife Service, Southeast Region, Atlanta, GA. 31 pp.

Hefner, J.M., B.O. Wilen, T.E. Dahl, and W.E. Frayer. 1994. Southeast Wetlands: Status and Trends, Mid-1970s to Mid-1980s. U.S. Department of the Interior, Fish and Wildlife Service, Atlanta, GA. 32 pp.

Stedman, S-M. and T.E. Dahl. 2008. Status and Trends of Wetlands in the Coastal Watersheds of the Eastern United States, 1998 to 2004. NOAA, National Marine Fisheries Service and U.S. Department of the Interior, Fish and Wildlife Service, Washington, DC. 32 pp.

Tiner, R. 2006. Salt Marsh Trends in Selected Estuaries of Southwestern Connecticut. NWI Cooperative Report, Northeast Region, Hadley, MA. Prepared for Long Island Sound Studies Program, Connecticut Department of Environmental Protection, Hartford, CT. 20 pp.

Tiner, R.W., J.Q. Swords, and H.C. Bergquist. 2005. Recent Wetland Trends in Southeastern Virginia: 1994-2000. U.S. Fish and Wildlife Service, National Wetlands Inventory, Northeast Region, Hadley, MA. NWI wetland trends report. 17 pp.

Tiner, R.W., J.Q. Swords, and H.C. Bergquist. 2005. Wetlands of the East of Hudson Watershed of the New York City Water Supply System: 2004 Status and Recent Trends (1994-2004). U.S. Fish and Wildlife Service, National Wetlands Inventory Program, Ecological Service, Region 5, Hadley, MA. Prepared for the New York City Department of Environmental Protection, Valhalla, NY. 63 pp.

Tiner, R.W., I.J. Huber, T. Nuerminger, and A.L. Mandeville. 2004. Coastal Wetland Trends in the Narragansett Bay Estuary During the 20th Century. U.S. Fish and Wildlife Service, Northeast Region, Hadley, MA. In cooperation with the University of Massachusetts-Amherst and the University of Rhode Island. National Wetlands Inventory Cooperative Interagency Report. 37 pp. plus appendices.

Tiner, R.W. and H.C. Bergquist. 2003. Historical Analysis of Wetlands and Their Functions for the Nanticoke River Watershed: A Comparison Between Pre-settlement and 1998 Conditions. U.S. Fish & Wildlife Service, National Wetlands Inventory (NWI) Program, Northeast Region, Hadley, MA. . NWI technical report. 38 pp. plus appendices and maps.

Tiner, R.W., J.Q. Swords, H.C. Bergquist, and G.P. DeAlessio. 2002. The Parker River Watershed: An Assessment of Recent Trends in Salt Marshes, Their Buffers, and River-Stream Buffer Zones (1985-1999). U.S. Fish and Wildlife Service, Northeast Region, Hadley, MA. National Wetlands Inventory Report. 20 pp.

Tiner, R.W., J.Q. Swords, and B.J. McClain. 2002. Wetland Status and Trends for the Hackensack Meadowlands. An Assessment Report from the U.S. Fish and Wildlife Service's National Wetlands Inventory Program. U.S. Fish and Wildlife Service, Northeast Region, Hadley, MA. 29 pp.

Tiner, R.W. 2001. Delaware's Wetlands: Status and Recent Trends. U.S. Fish and Wildlife Service, Hadley, MA. Prepared for the Delaware Department of Natural Resources and Environmental Control, Watershed Assessment Section, Division of Water Resources, Dover, DE. Cooperative National Wetlands Inventory publication. 19 pp.

Tiner, R.W., I. Kenenski, T. Nuerminger, D.B. Foulis, J. Eaton, G.S. Smith, and W.E. Frayer. 1994. Recent Wetland Status and Trends in the Chesapeake Watershed (1982 to 1989): Technical Report. Chesapeake Bay Program, Annapolis, MD. 70 pp. plus appendices.

Tiner, R.W., Jr. 1987. Mid-Atlantic Wetlands: A Disappearing Natural Treasure. U.S. Fish and Wildlife Service, Region 5, Newton Corner, MA and U.S. Environmental Protection Agency, Region III, Philadelphia, PA. Cooperative public information booklet. 28 pp.

Tiner, R.W., Jr., and J.T. Finn. 1986. Status and Recent Trends of Wetlands in Five Mid-Atlantic States: Delaware, Maryland, Pennsylvania, Virginia, and West Virginia. U.S. Fish and Wildlife Service, Region 5, National Wetlands Inventory Project, Newton Corner, MA and U.S. Environmental Protection Agency, Region III, Philadelphia, PA. Cooperative publication. 40 pp.

Tiner, R., J. Swords, and S. Schaller. 1999. Wetland Trends in the Croton Watershed, New York: 1960s to 1990s. U.S. Fish and Wildlife Service, Ecological Services, Northeast Region, Hadley, MA. Prepared for N.Y. City Department of Environmental Protection, Bureau of Water Supply, Quality and Protection, Valhalla, NY. 24 pp.

Tiner, R.W., D.B. Foulis, C. Nichols, S. Schaller, D. Petersen, K. Andersen, and J. Swords. 1998. Wetland Status and Recent Trends for the Neponset Watershed, Massachusetts (1977-1991). U.S. Fish and Wildlife Service, Ecological Services, National Wetlands Inventory Program, Northeast Region, Hadley, MA. Prepared for the Massachusetts Department of Environmental Protection, Bureau of Resource Protection, Worcester, MA and the U.S. Army Corps of Engineers, New England District, Concord, MA. 28 pp.

Tiner, R.W., and D.B. Foulis. 1992. Wetland Trends in Prince Georges County, Maryland From 1981 to 1988-90. U.S. Fish and Wildlife Service, Hadley, MA. 15 pp.

Tiner, R.W., J. Stone, and J. Gookin. 1989. Current Status and Recent Trends in Wetlands of Central Connecticut. Prepared for the U.S. Environmental Protection Agency, Boston, MA. U.S. Fish and Wildlife Service, Newton Corner, MA. 9 pp.

Tiner, R.W., Jr., and W. Zinni, Jr. 1988. Recent Wetland Trends in Southeastern Massachusetts. Prepared for the U.S. Army Corps of Engineers, New England Division, Waltham, MA. U.S. Fish and Wildlife Service, Newton Corner, MA. 9 pp.

Wetland Characterization and Functional Assessment Reports

Tiner, R.W. and H.C. Bergquist. 2007. The Hackensack River Watershed, New Jersey/New York Wetland Characterization, Preliminary Assessment of Wetland Functions, and Remotely-sensed Assessment of Natural Habitat Integrity. U.S. Fish and Wildlife Service, National Wetlands Inventory, Ecological Services, Region 5, Hadley, MA. 134 pp.

Tiner, R.W. 2006. Wetlands of the Cumberland Bay Watershed, Clinton County, New York. U.S. Fish and Wildlife Service, National Wetlands Inventory, Northeast Region, Hadley, MA. Prepared for the New York State Department of Environmental Conservation, Division of Fish, Wildlife, and Marine Resources, Bureau of Habitat, Albany, NY. 25 pp.

Tiner, R.W. 2006. Wetlands of the Upper Wappinger Creek Watershed, Dutchess County, New York. U.S. Fish and Wildlife Service, National Wetlands Inventory, Northeast Region, Hadley, MA. Prepared for the New York State Department of Environmental Conservation, Division of Fish, Wildlife, and Marine Resources, Bureau of Habitat, Albany, NY. 21 pp.

Tiner, R.W. and J. Stewart. 2004. Wetland Characterization and Preliminary Assessment of Wetland Functions for the Delaware and Catskill Watersheds of the New York City Water Supply System. U.S. Fish and Wildlife Service, National Wetlands Inventory, Ecological Services, Region 5, Hadley, MA. Prepared for the New York City Department of Environmental Protection, Valhalla, NY. 50 pp. plus appendices.

Tiner, R.W. 2003. Correlating Enhanced National Wetlands Inventory Data with Wetland Functions for Watershed Assessments: A Rationale for Northeastern U.S. Wetlands. U.S. Fish and Wildlife Service, National Wetlands Inventory Program, Northeast Region, Hadley, MA. 26 pp.

Tiner, R.W., H.C. Bergquist, J.Q. Swords, and B.J. McClain. 2001. Watershed-based Wetland Characterization for Delaware's Nanticoke River Watershed: A Preliminary Assessment Report. U.S. Fish and Wildlife Service, Ecological Services, National Wetlands Inventory Program, Northeast Region, Hadley, MA. Prepared for Delaware Department of Natural Resources and Environmental Control, Division of Soil and Water Conservation, Dover, DE. 89 pp. plus 22 maps.

Tiner, R., M. Starr, H. Bergquist, and J. Swords. 2000. Watershed-based Wetland Characterization for Maryland's Nanticoke River and Coastal Bays Watersheds: A Preliminary Assessment Report. U.S. Fish and Wildlife Service, Ecological Services, National Wetlands Inventory Program, Northeast Region, Hadley, MA. Prepared for Maryland Department of Natural Resources, Annapolis, MD. 75 pp. plus appendices.

Tiner, R., S. Schaller, D. Petersen, K. Snider, K. Ruhlman, and J. Swords. 1999. Wetland Characterization Study and Preliminary Assessment of Wetland Functions for the Casco Bay Watershed, Southern Maine. U.S. Fish and Wildlife Service, Ecological Services, Northeast Region, Hadley, MA. Prepared for the Maine State Planning Office, Augusta, ME. 51 pp. plus appendices.

Wetland Restoration Inventories

Tiner, R.W., I.J. Huber, T. Nuerminger, and A.L. Mandeville. 2003. An Inventory of Coastal Wetlands, Potential Coastal Restoration Sites, Wetland Buffers, and Hardened Shorelines for the Narragansett Bay Estuary. U.S. Fish and Wildlife Service, Northeast Region, Hadley, MA. Prepared for the Rhode Island Department of Environmental Management, Narragansett Bay Estuary Program, Providence, RI. National Wetlands Inventory Cooperative Interagency Report. 41 pp. plus appendices.

Tiner, R., I. Huber, and M. Starr. 2001. Wetlands and Potential Wetland Restoration Sites for the Upper Ipswich Watershed. U.S. Fish and Wildlife Service, Ecological Services, Northeast Region, Hadley, MA in cooperation with the University of Massachusetts, Natural Resources Assessment Group, Department of Plant and Soil Sciences, Amherst, MA. National Wetlands Inventory Report prepared for the Massachusetts Wetlands Restoration & Banking Program, Executive Office of Environmental Affairs, Boston, MA. 17 pp. plus appendices.

Tiner, R., J. Swords, I. Huber, T. Nuerminger, and M. Starr. 2000. Wetlands and Potential Wetland Restoration Sites for the Mill Rivers and Manhan River Watersheds. U.S. Fish and Wildlife Service, Ecological Services, Northeast Region, Hadley, MA. National Wetlands Inventory Report prepared for the U.S. Army Corps of Engineers, New England District, Concord, MA. 19 pp. plus appendices.

Special Topic Reports

Dahl, T.E. 1990. Wetlands Losses in the United States 1780's to 1980's. U.S. Department of the Interior, Fish and Wildlife Service, Washington, DC. 13 pp.

Tiner, R.W., H.C. Bergquist, G.P. DeAlessio, and M.J. Starr. 2002. Geographically Isolated Wetlands: A Preliminary Assessment of Their Characteristics and Status in Selected Areas of the United States. U.S. Department of the Interior, Fish and Wildlife Service, Hadley, MA. CD and web-based report. 270 pp.

Tiner, R.W., and G.S. Smith. 1992. Comparison of Four Scales of Color Infrared Photography for Wetland Mapping in Maryland. U.S. Fish and Wildlife Service, Region 5, Fish and Wildlife Enhancement, Newton Corner, MA. Misc. National Wetlands Inventory Report. 14 pp. plus tables.

APPENDIX B: List of Contributors to the NWI
(Primary Source: Jo Ann Mills, USFWS, Washington Office, with review and additions from Regional Wetland Coordinators)

Federal Agencies

Air Force
Air National Guard
Army
Army Corps of Engineers
Coast Guard
Navy
USDA Forest Service
USDA Natural Resource Conservation Service
Department of Energy
DOI Bureau of Indian Affairs
DOI Bureau of Land Management
DOI Bureau of Reclamation
DOI Fish and Wildlife Service
DOI Geological Survey
DOI National Park Service
Environmental Protection Agency
Department of Housing and Urban Development
Department of Transportation
Tennessee Valley Authority

States or State Agencies

Alabama Geological Survey*
Alaska Fish and Game
Alaska Department of Transportation
Arizona Department of Environmental Quality
Arizona Game and Fish
Arkansas Multi-Agency Wetland Planning Team
California Resources Agency
Colorado Division of Wildlife
Colorado Natural Heritage Program
Connecticut Department of Environmental Protection
Delaware Department of Natural Resources and Environmental Control
Florida Department of Environmental Regulation
Florida Department of Natural Resources
Georgia Department of Natural Resources
Georgia Geological Survey
Hawaii Division of Forestry and Wildlife*
Hawaii Office of Environmental Quality
Idaho Fish and Game
Illinois Natural History Survey
Indiana Department of Natural Resources
Iowa Department of Natural Resources
Kansas Water Office
Kentucky Department of Fish and Wildlife Resources
Kentucky Natural Resources and Environmental Protection*
Louisiana Geological Survey*
Maine Geological Survey*
Maine Office of GIS
Maine State Planning Office
Maine Land Use Regulation Commission
Maryland Department of Natural Resources
Maryland Geological Survey*

Massachusetts Executive Office of Environmental Affairs
Michigan Department of Natural Resources
Minnesota Department of Natural Resources
Mississippi Department of Marine Resources
Missouri Department of Conservation
Montana Department of Environmental Quality
Montana Department of Transportation
Montana Fish and Wildlife and Parks
Montana Natural Heritage Program
Nebraska Conservation Survey Division
Nebraska Game and Parks
Nevada Department of Environmental Protection
New Hampshire Office of State Planning*
New Jersey Department of Environmental Protection
New York Department of Environmental Conservation
North Carolina Center for Geographic Information and Analysis
North Carolina Department of Environment, Health, and Natural Resources*
North Carolina Department of Natural Resources
Ohio Department of Natural Resources*
Oklahoma Conservation Commission
Oklahoma Water Resources Board*
Oregon Department of Energy
Oregon Department of State Lands
Oregon Watershed Enhancement Board
Pennsylvania Department of Environmental Protection
Puerto Rico Department of Natural Resources and Environmental Management
Rhode Island Department of Environmental Management
South Carolina Department of Natural Resources
South Carolina Land Resources Commission
South Carolina Water Resources Commission
South Dakota Game, Fish and Parks
Tennessee Wildlife Resources Agency
U.S. Virgin Islands Department of Planning and Natural Resources
Utah Natural Resources
Vermont Department of Environmental Conservation*
Virginia Department of Conservation and Recreation
Virginia Department of Game and Inland Fisheries
Washington Department of Ecology
Washington Department of Natural Resources
Washington Department of Wildlife
West Virginia Department of Natural Resources
Wyoming Game and Fish Department
Wyoming Department of Environmental Quality

Native American Tribes

Coeur d'Alene Tribe (Idaho)
Confederated Salish and Kootenai Tribes (Montana)
Fond du Lac Band of Lake Superior Chippewa Tribe (Minnesota)
Hoopa Valley Tribe (California)
Navajo Nation (Arizona)
Yurok Tribe (California)

Regional or Local Governments

Anchorage Borough (AK)
City and County of Denver (CO)
El Paso County (CO)
Fairbanks North Star Borough (AK)
Kent County Conservation District (DE)
Lewis and Clark County (MT)
Matanuska-Susitna Borough (AK)
Mecklenberg County (NC)

New York City Department of Environmental Protection (NY)
North Slope Borough (AK)
Portland METRO (OR)
Orange County (NC)
Seattle Department of Planning and Development (WA)
South Florida Water Management District (FL)
Southwest Florida Water Management District (FL)
St. Johns Water Management District (FL)
Suffolk County (NY)
Tompkins County (NY)
Ulster County (NY)

Universities

California State Universities
Cornell University*
Florida State University*
Northern Illinois University*
Oklahoma State University
San Francisco State University
South Dakota State University
St. Mary's University (Minnesota)
Texas Tech University
University of Alaska
University of Arizona
University of Florida
University of Georgia*
University of Minnesota*
University of Massachusetts
University of Nebraska*
University of Oklahoma
University of Texas
University of the Virgin Islands
Virginia Polytechnic Institute and State University (Virginia Tech)

Map distribution center only

U.S. Fish & Wildlife Service
http://www.fws.gov

National Wetlands Inventory
http://www.fws.gov/wetlands

Division of Habitat and Resource Conservation
http://www.fws.gov/habitatconservation

October 2009

Cover photograph of a wetland in Maine
by Ralph Tiner/U.S. Fish and Wildlife Service